KARGIL

KARGIL

THE HEIGHTS OF BRAVERY

AZAD SINGH RATHORE

PARTRIDGE

To order additional copies of this book, contact
Partridge India
000 800 10062 62
orders.india@partridgepublishing.com

www.partridgepublishing.com/india

CONTENTS

<u>To The Brave Soldiers of Indian Army</u>

हालात कितने भी मुश्किल क्यों न हो
दुश्मन कितना भी मज़बूत क्यों न हो

आंच जब मादरे - वतन की इज्ज़त पर आ जाये
तो हमारी शिराओं में बहते हुए लहू का वेग
ज्वालामुखी से भी प्रचंड होता है ।

हालात दोज़ख से भी दुश्वार थे
ज़मीन के फ़िरदौस में
तब हिन्द की सेना ने
युद्धों के इतिहास में कारगिल का नाम
अदम्य साहस, शौर्य और पराक्रम से लिखा था ।

Times may be trying,
Enemy may be fierce;

When honour of the motherland is at strike;
Then, blood in our veins boils like ferocious volcano!!

When predicament was worse than hell in the *heaven - on – Earth*
Then, Indian soldiers inscribed name of Kargil in the history of battles
with their indomitable spirit of courage, valour and bravery.˙

*   These beautiful lines dedicated to soldiers of Indian Army are written by Revant Dan ji Barath (Bhinyad) and translated in english by Kailash Dan ji Ratnoo (Koda).

PREFACE

After its independence, India was forced to fight five battles with its neighbouring countries because of their aggression in our territories. India fought one war with China (1962) and four with Pakistan (1947, 1965, 1971, 1999). I heard so many stories about these battles at my maternal grandfather's place in Sikar—where I spent my entire student life at my maternal grandfather's home. Sikar belongs to Rajasthan's Shekhawati region, a place that claims a very high number of its residents serving in the Indian Army as soldiers and officers in Rajasthan.

Stories of bravery of the Indian Army are widely told and listened here with immense pride. My childhood was spent surrounded by all these kind of stories everywhere. Most of the members of my maternal grandfather's family served in armed forces. Both of my maternal uncles served in prestigious and elite force, SPG and NSG.

I was 16 at the time of Kargil War. My teenage mind was very much affected by this war. Hearing all about the war, stories of brave soldiers sacrificing their life for the respect of our country, deep within the corner of my mind, I, too, at times thought to join the Indian Army. Today, it has been years since we fought Kargil War, but the stories of it still plays a significant role in inspiring the school and college students.

Although there are many respected authors who have beautifully narrated this story in their writings, I felt the need for a book, which could retell this glorious piece of history in easy words and easy narratives. A book which could explain Indian Army's glory to people and especially youth of this country, so that our present and coming generation can read about sacrifice and courage of our soldiers, feel proud about the Indian Army, and the assault operations of our brave soldiers who defended our motherland by throwing out enemy from heights of Kargil region. Today, because of them, we are enjoying our freedom and peace. I also want readers to know the main reasons of Pakistan's aggression in our territory, its bad intensions and planning behind Kargil War, and about our excellent diplomacy, which helped our soldiers in winning this war and keeping sovereignty of our country untouched.

By inspiration of my friends, I dared to write about this glorious past, Kargil. I have always had keen interest in defence related books and documentaries, but I never imagined that I would write a defence related book. This is my first book I am writing as an author, so it is obvious that it was very challenging but interesting experience. Initially, it was very difficult for me to put whole event and research on paper, as I never did this before. But very soon after I started, everything went in flow.

I enjoyed the research, reading so many books and articles on subject, and discussing the event with my army friends and war reporters over mail, telephone, and face to face. I hope, as a reader, you will find this book informative and interesting.

ACKNOWLEDGEMENT

First time I am writing a book, and it's very obvious that I am feeling a mixture of many emotions while writing this part of it. I will not let go this opportunity without mentioning those who have a great significance in my life and inspired me in writing this book.

First and foremost, I would like to give my regards to *Jeesa and Bhabhu* (my paternal grandparents) and *Nanosa and Nanisa* (my maternal grandparents). I am thankful for their love and blessings.

A very special thanks to my *Nanosa* who is the first teacher and mentor of my life; he taught me the value of hard work and persistence. I would like to thank my parents for giving me this beautiful life, helping me realise my own potential, and making me the person I am. Thanks are due to my brother, *Siddharth*, and my cousin brothers and sisters. I owe more than I can ever express to my wife, *Jyotsna*. The support she has provided me over the years is the greatest gift I could ever get. I am thankful to her for bringing her lady luck to my life and giving me two beautiful angels—our daughters, *Shivranjani* and *Divyaranjani*. Handling three children (including me being the most childish one) at home must have a huge task.

I would like to express my heartfelt gratitude to *Manvedra Singh ji* and *Chitra Bhabhisa* for giving me their love and treating me as a part of their own family.

I remain deeply indebted to *Hema Ram ji Choudhary, Sanjay Dixit ji*, and *Devaram ji Choudhary* for having faith in me.

I have always enjoyed the love and affection of my uncles who pampered me well during my childhood (and they still do). I am thankful to them for so many things, from teaching me how to ride a scooter, driving a jeep, receiving pocket money for travelling, and especially saving me from angry rebukes of my father. I shall always remain thankful to *Ishwer Singh, Shyam Singh, Surendra Singh, Papsa kaku, Lal ji kaku (Maadsaab), Sumer Singh, Shambhu Kaku, Dipendra Singh, Narpat Kaku, and Mahipal Singh (Chilly)* for treating me in such an exquisite fashion. I owe a debt of gratitude to my father-in-law, *Bhanwar Singh ji*, and entire *Khuri* family, especially my brothers-in-law for giving me much respect and affection.

At this juncture, I would like to spend a moment to remember my friend, *Late Dr Virendra Choudhary*. He will always be missed. I would also like to extend my gratefulness to my friends, *Mohan Choudhary, Sudhanshu Jangid, Vijay Choudhary, Rajendra Singh, Narayan Singh, and Jaidev* for giving me brotherly love and being with me in all the good and bad times of my life. I am also thankful to *Dharam Singh Bhati, Revant Dan ji, Sunder Dan ji, Bhupesh Aacharya and Dev Bhadu fo*r giving me confidence to write this book.

I am thankful *to Kalyan, Pratap Singh,* and *Ajeet Singh,* Niranjan- brothers from my extended *Rathore* family, for giving me their affection and the delightful moments we shared and time we spent together. I would like to thank all members of *Marwar Riders* - My motorbike riding group

I am so much thankful to CAIRN INDIA Ltd and its associate companies for opening the door of opportunities to start and enables me to explore business possibilities in my own hometown, Barmer, a small and sleepy city that lies in western part of Rajasthan. I am grateful to Raja Chelliah and Abhijit Singh for showing trust and believing my entrepreneurship skill at the time when I was in only early twenties and a newcomer in field of business.

Speaking of encouragement, I must mention my friends in Indian Army, *Col Mahendra Tiwari, Maj Ankush Pratap Singh, Maj Adhiraj Singh, Maj Sudhanshu Khurana, and Maj Ashwini Singh Rana* for supporting me. They are the one who inspired me to write this book.

I highly appreciate the tireless efforts of *Abhishek Choudhary* and my office staff, especially *Devendra Joshi and Rahul Khatri* for providing me study material, data, and valuable inputs while working on manuscript.

I have a deep respect for the authors and writers of books, thesis, essays, and articles, which I had read to understand the situation and incidents that transpired during the Kargil War.

I am thankful to Partridge Publications and their team for helping me to polish the manuscript. Without them, this book would never find its way to the massive world of printing.

Last, but definitely not the least, I ask forgiveness of all those who have been with me and blessed me with their love and support over the course of the years, and whose names I may have failed to mention.

FOREWORD

by Manvendra Singh

Through human history there have been some wars, battles, that over time become essentials of folklore. Military history transforms into popular culture, tales of heroism become pegs in the identification of national landmarks. Over time they come to define national culture, national identity and come handy in making statements of pride. National folklore revolves around these gallant actions and battles, to evolve into statements of case. These are defining moments in national growth, of character, of resolve and resilience. As they get passed down from generation to generation these events develop a momentum and mass of their own, and thus grow into something larger then they may have been in the first instance. May have been, since some of the battles through history have been enormously important in any case.

The siege of Stalingrad during the Second World War, and the enormous sacrifices made by the Russian people in reversing Nazi Germany's successes, is as momentous an event as there can be. And so it continues to reverberate in the Russian national psyche. It's impact on the national make up cannot be underestimated. The Opium Wars on Chinese national thinking is a case in reverse. Where the defeat of a people, and the advancement of colonialism, is held as the example of something that cannot be allowed to happen again. Then there is the Boer War in South African history, which really cemented an identity for Afrikaans as an independent people. And from the Second Boer War came the Battle of Spion Kop the impact of which continues to be felt in United Kingdom till today, for the name is still used in a village and a number of sporting facilities. The most famous of which is of course the Kop End at Anfield, home Liverpool Football Club.

A similar impact of a battle on national psyche is that of the Battle of Kargil vis-a-vis India. It has come to define the epitome of Indian resolve and determination. That it was the best example of military and diplomatic operations ever undertaken by India is an important aside. Just the fact that it happened, and the manner in which it took place, puts it up there in Indian pride of place. I recall, barely a few days into the campaign, when it wasn't even clear who the intruders were, an officer holding an important appointment in Army Hqs, New Delhi, telling me that India would never be able to evict the intrusion before summer came to an end, and that it was the end of Kargil as Indian territory. I instinctively told him that there was no choice but to evict the intrusions for that was what the nation demanded. I hold no claim to being a military soothsayer, but was merely voicing public murmurs. Well the murmurs became loud enough for them to become a tail wind that helped brave young officers and soldiers evict intruders who occupied the dominating heights. It was a military first in history, and rightly became the battle that has come define Indian determination.

The fact that it has had an almost opposite impact on the Pakistani psyche is not a coincidence, for that was how it all began, with deceit. So there is an underlying guilt in Pakistan, and an overwhelming pride in India. The result of which is that there is a dearth of writing in Pakistan about why, how and what happened in Kargil. The guilt is far too deep, and the shame continues to impact on the Pakistan Army. So whatever writing there is, is few and far in between. In India, on the other hand, there has been much written about Kargil. From newspaper stories, to racy journalistic accounts, and to dense military historical series, India has been served all options. From thrillers to heavy reading everything is available. There was a gap in between, and an important one at that.

What does an average reader do? An average reader being one who has the curiosity to know what happened in Kargil, why did it happen, it's background, and it's outcome. And the average reader wants it in simple language, without difficult military jargon, and media name dropping. The average reader wants something that can become a reference point, material for the young and old who are looking for a book that can be constantly used as a ready reckoner. Azad Singh has provided just that book, simple, to the point, without jargon, and which packs in all important details. A school child would find it as beneficial as an accomplished adult looking to refresh memory. For the Battle for Kargil is something that is never going to leave Indian memories.

Manvendra Singh *represented Barmer in the 14ᵗʰ Lok Sabha, where he was a member of the Standing Committee on Defence. Before entering politics, he worked as a journalist at the Statesman and the Indian Express, with a specialization in defence and national security affairs. During the Kargil War, as an army officer, he worked very closely with Chief of Army Staff as his Public Relation Officer (Army) and Media Adviser. Presently he is a Member of Legislative Assembly from Shiv constituency for Rajasthan Vidhan Sabha.*

CHAPTER 1

JAMMU AND KASHMIR

'Gar firdaus bur ruh-e-zamin ast, hamin asto, hamin asto, hamin ast.'*

(If there is a heaven on earth, it's here, it's here, it's only here.)

CHAPTER 1

Jammu and Kashmir is a state of India, situated in northern region. It is often denoted by acronym J&K.

Jammu and Kashmir shares its international border with China in east, Pakistan in west, Afghanistan in north. It shares domestic border with Punjab and Himachal Pradesh. The State of Jammu and Kashmir is stretched between 32° 17' N to 37°–05' of northern latitude and 72°–31' to 80° 20' of east longitude. From north to south, it's extended 640 kilometres in length, and from east to west over 480 kilometres in breadth.

The State of Jammu and Kashmir became a part of the Mughal Empire under Akbar from 1586. Earlier, it had been under the kingdom of Hindu kings and Muslim sultans. It came under the reign of the Sikh Kingdom of Punjab in 1819 after a period of Afghan rule from 1756. Maharaja Ranjit Singh of Punjab kingdom handed over the territory, Jammu, to Gulab Singh in 1820. Later in 1846, under the treaty of Amritsar, Kashmir was also handed over to Gulab Singh. Ladakh was added in 1830. Thus, this was the biggest princely state (with a total area of 2,22,236 sq km) found by Maharaja Gulab Singh in 1846 until the partition of the country in August, 1947.

In August 1947, Britishers announced independence to British administrated India by separating it in two countries, India and Pakistan. Just after the independence announced by the Britishers, Pakistan invaded the Kashmir in October 1947 to claim it illegally. Maharaja Hari Singh was last ruler of Kashmir princely state. After independence he was left with a choice to join India or Pakistan. Though required to choose between India and Pakistan the Maharaja was unable to decide which state to join or become an independent state without joining any of them. Newly made Pakistan wanted Kashmir in its territory. Tensions between Pakistan and the government of Kashmir grew as the Maharaja's indecision frustrated Pakistan and pro-Pakistani factions within

Kashmir. Hostilities began in early October 1947 when a tribal rebellion broke out in Poonch in southwest Kashmir. By October 20th the Pakistani army entered the conflict in support of the tribal forces in a multi-pronged effort designed to capture Uri, Jhangar, Rajuara, and Naushera in the opening days of the campaign.

Famous writer and associate professor at the Center for Peace and Security Studies (CPASS) C. Christine Fair notes that this was the beginning of Pakistan using irregular forces and 'asymmetric warfare' to ensure plausible deniability, which has continued ever since.

Pakistan's timetable was to capture the capital of Kashmir, Srinagar, within a week. The Maharaja had already fled his capital, Srinagar, to seek the comparative safety of Jammu. The Maharaja, facing overwhelming odds and near certain defeat, asked India for military support. India agreed to provide help on condition that Kashmir acceded to India and that the Maharaja of Kashmir agreed to the accession. The Maharaja of Kashmir agreed to these terms and on October 26 the Maharaja Hari Singh signed the Instrument of accession (See Appendix -I Instrument of Accession of Jammu and Kashmir). Indian army reached Srinagar and started throwing back intruders from Kashmir valley.

India put this issue 'aggression of Pakistan in Indian territory' at United Nations, and sought resolution of the issue at the UN Security Council in following UN intervention that resulted in ceasefire between both countries. Indian forces retaliated, but area measuring 76,898 sq km (i.e., Mirpur, Kotli, and some parts of Poonch and Northern area) consisted of Gilgit and '*frontier Illaqas*' of Hunja, and nearby areas remained under Pakistan's occupation, leaving 141,338.2 sq km on the Indian side. The ground position at the time of ceasefire is called ceasefire line (CFL). United Nations passed a resolution to resolve the situation (See Appendix II, Resolution 47, 1948, on the India-Pakistan question submitted jointly by the representatives for Belgium, Canada, China, Colombia, the United Kingdom, and United States of America, and adopted by the security council at its 286th meeting held on 21 April 1948).

Resolution and Mediation

India lodged a complaint under Article 35 (Chapter VI) of the UN Charter in the UN Security Council on 1 January 1948, charging Pakistan with 'aiding and abetting' the Pakistani tribal invasion in Jammu and Kashmir.

In the United Nations, India claimed that all the territories of the Princely State of Jammu and Kashmir legally belonged to India by virtue of the treaty of accession signed by the king of the kingdom with the Indian Union, as India took this matter of aggression of Pakistani Army to Indian territory at the UN security council. UN set up a commission, UNITED NATIONS COMMISSION FOR INDIA AND PAKISTAN (UNCIP), to resolve the situation. In the following, UN Security Council passed the resolution 47 (See Appendix-II UN Resolution 47)on 21 April 1948. UN called for immediate ceasefire and told the government of Pakistan to secure the withdrawal from State of Jammu and Kashmir of tribesmen, and Pakistan nationals not normally resident therein who have entered the state for the purpose of fighting. On 1 January 1949, India and Pakistan signed an agreement for ceasefire and to respect UN resolution. However, Pakistan refused to follow the UN resolution and kept its control over a large part of Jammu and Kashmir, which is presently known as, Pakistan occupied Kashmir (POK), actually a part of INDIA.

Summary of Resolution Adopted by UN Nations
Resolution Adopted by the United Nations Commission for India and Pakistan on 13 August 1948

THE UNITED NATIONS COMMISSION FOR INDIA AND PAKISTAN
Having given careful consideration to the points of view expressed by the representatives of India and Pakistan regarding the situation in the State of Jammu and Kashmir, and being of the opinion that the prompt cessation of hostilities and the correction of conditions the continuance of which is likely to endanger international peace and security, are essential to implementation of its endeavours to assist the governments of India and Pakistan in effecting a final settlement of the situation, resolves to submit simultaneously to the governments of India and Pakistan with the following proposal.

PART I
CEASE-FIRE ORDER

[A] The governments of India and Pakistan agree that their respective high commands will issue separately and simultaneously a ceasefire order to apply to all forces under their control in the State of Jammu and Kashmir as of the earliest practisable date or dates to be mutually agreed upon within four days after these proposals have been accepted by both governments.

[B] The high commands of Indian and Pakistan forces agree to refrain from taking any measures that might augment the military potential of the forces under their control in the State of Jammu and Kashmir. (For the purpose of these proposals, forces under their control shall be considered to include all forces, unorganised groups, fighting or participating in hostilities on their respective sides).

[C] The commanders-in-chief of the Forces of India and Pakistan shall promptly confer regarding any necessary local changes in present dispositions, which may facilitate the ceasefire.

[D] In its discretion, and as the commission may find practisable, the commission will appoint military observers who was under the authority of the commission, and with the cooperation of both commands will supervise the observance of the ceasefire order.

[E] The government of India and the government of Pakistan agree to appeal to their respective people to assist in creating and maintaining an atmosphere favourable to the promotion of further negotiations.

PART II
TRUCE AGREEMENT

Simultaneously, with the acceptance of the proposal for the immediate cessation of hostilities as outlined in part one, both governments accept the following principles as a basis for the formulation of a truce agreement, the details of which shall be worked out in discussion between their representatives and the commission.

A.

(1) As the presence of troops of Pakistan in the territory of the State of Jammu and Kashmir constitutes a material change in the situation since it was represented by the government of Pakistan before the security council. The government of Pakistan agrees to withdraw its troops from that state.

(2) The government of Pakistan will use its best endeavour to secure the withdrawal from the State of Jammu and Kashmir of tribesmen and

Pakistan nationals not normally resident therein who have entered the state for the purpose of fighting.

(3) Pending a final solution, the territory evacuated by the Pakistan troops will be administered by the local authorities under the surveillance of the commission.

B.

(1) When the commission shall have notified the government of India that the tribesmen and Pakistan nationals—referred to in PART II, A(2)—hereof have withdrawn, thereby terminating the situation, which was represented by the government of India to the security council as having occasioned the presence of Indian forces in the State of Jammu and Kashmir; and further, that the Pakistan forces are being withdrawn from the State of Jammu and Kashmir. The government of India agrees to begin to withdraw the bulk of their forces from the state in stages to be agreed upon with the commission.

(2) Pending the acceptance of the conditions for a final settlement of the situation in the State of Jammu and Kashmir, Indian Government will maintain within the lines existing at the moment of ceasefire the minimum strength of its forces which, in agreement with the commission, are considered necessary to assist local authorities in the observance of law and order. The commission will have observers stationed where it deems necessary.

(3) The government of India will undertake to ensure that the government of the State of Jammu and Kashmir will take all measures within their power to make it publicly known that peace, law, and order will be safeguarded, and that all human and political rights will be guaranteed.

C.

(1) Upon signature, the full text of the truce agreement, or communique containing the principles thereof as agreed upon between the two governments and the commission, will be made public.

PART III

The government of India and the government of Pakistan reaffirm their wish that the future status of the State of Jammu and Kashmir shall be determined in accordance with the will of the people; and to that end, upon acceptance of the truce agreement, both governments agree to enter into consultations with the commission to determine fair and equitable conditions whereby such free expression will be assured. The UNCIP unanimously adopted this Resolution on 13-8-1948. Members of the commission: Argentina, Belgium, Colombia, Czechoslovakia, and USA.

In following years, in 1962, China occupied a bigger area of Ladakh and Pakistan—also illegally ceded same area of its occupied Kashmir to China. This area is known as Aksai Chin.

Present Jammu and Kashmir

As I mentioned above, areas occupied by Pakistan on other side of Cease Fire Line (CFL) are known as Pakistan Occupied Kashmir or POK. Later, after 1971 India-Pakistan War CFL was replaced by Line of Control (LOC) in agreement between India and Pakistan known as 1972 Shimla Agreement. At present, LOC or Line of Control denotes a kind of boundary separating the Jammu and Kashmir in two parts—Jammu and Kashmir and part of Kashmir region illegally controlled by Pakistan (POK). LOC is nearly about 435 miles or 700 kilometre long. Details about LOC and Shimla agreement are mentioned in following chapter.

After signing of accession by Maharaja Hari Singh, the State of Jammu and Kashmir was found on 26 October 1947. The state has given special autonomy under article 370 of Indian Constitution. Srinagar is summer, and Jammu is winter capital of state. Majority population in state is Muslim.

The State of Jammu and Kashmir, bestowed with lofty snow mountains, fascinating valleys, sparkling streams, rushing rivers, and lush forests. People all over the world admire its picturesque landscape and snow covered mountains. The state is very famous for its wildlife and lush jungles. It is very famous among the visitors, those who are keen to visit holy places. There are various attractions for a visitor in Jammu and Kashmir, which includes historic places, beautiful landscapes, never-ending lush forests, and some rare wildlife that is only found here.

Jammu and Kashmir is the home of spirituality. The place has been a favourite among saints for centuries. One can say that it is a place that is blessed by gods. Its beauty is further enhanced by its beautiful rivers, crystal clear calm lakes, picturesque waterfalls, and the cypress trees that are found here in abundance. Jammu and Kashmir is also famous for ancient Mughal heritage and Hindu shrines. Jammu and Kashmir has always been a favourite destination for domestic, as well as foreign tourist. Tourism is main source of revenue for the government of Jammu and Kashmir. Industry was badly hit because of insurgency, and presently is in worst phase. Disturbed tourism industry also affected economic condition of local people. Mostly foreign tourists avoid visiting this heaven on earth because of terrorist attacks. However, the attraction of pilgrims and devotees toward Hindu Shrines and Buddhist Monastery is nevertheless and keep attracting the domestic tourist to state.

It is this long and living culture link of people of India that Pakistan has sought to destroy through Jehad in the name of Islamic fundamentalism.

Jammu and Kashmir consists of **three divisions**: Jammu, Kashmir Valley, and Ladakh and is further divided into twenty-two districts. The Siachen Glacier, although under Indian military control, does not lie under the administration of the State of Jammu and Kashmir.

DIST	22
No. of Tehsil	82
Blocks	143
Panchayat	4128

Source http://nidm.gov.in/pdf/dp/Jammu.pdf

Jammu Division

Jammu, Kathua, Udhampur, Poonch, Rajouri, Doda, Kishtwar, Ramban, Reasi, and Samba are districts in Jammu division. The main language of Jammu region is Dogri, Pahari, Punjabi, and some Kashmiri speaking people in Doda district. Majority of population is Hindu in this region (about 66.3 per cent). However, Doda, Poonch, and Rajouri have a Muslim majority. Pir Panjal range separates Jammu from Kashmir Valley. The climate of region varies with altitude. The average high temperature is 38.7º C and low is 7.8º C in last thirty years.

Kashmir Division

Srinagar, Budgam, Anantnag, Pulwama, Baramulla, Kupwara, Bandipur, Ganderbal, Kulgam, and Shopian are the districts in Srinagar division. The main language is Kashmiri and *Gujari*. Muslims are in majority in this region with a minority of Kashmiri Pandits. Most of Muslims in valley are Sunni, while areas laying over LOC are Shia majority. Kashmir Valley has a moderate climate with the towering Kara Koram range in the north, Pir Panjal in south, and Zanskar range in the east. It can be generally described as cool in spring, mild in summer, and very cold in winter. Hottest month is July (about 6° C to 32° C), and coolest is December (about -15° C to 0° C)

Ladakh Division

Kargil and Leh are districts in Ladakh Division. Ladakh is known as arctic cold region—coolest area of India. Bhoti is main language in the region. Weather here is extreme, remains mostly chilly and cold throughout year. Heavy snowfalls, landslides, avalanche are very common; thus, making it a very inhospitable for living. In winter, temperature goes close to -40° C. This was the region where Kargil was fought in summers of 1999. Dras, a town and mostly affected area of Kargilwar, is world's second coldest habitant. Siachin is coldest and highest battleground in the world, also a part of this region.

Division	Area km²	Percentage Area
Kashmir	22374.9 sq km	15.83%
Jammu	32058.8 sq km	22.68%
Ladakh	86904.4 sq km	61.49%
Total area of three Divisions of Jammu and Kashmir	141338.2 sq km	100%

Source http://nidm.gov.in/pdf/dp/Jammu.pdf

Kashmir Valley, Tawi Valley, Chenab Valley, Sindh Valley, Lidder Valley, and Mushkoh Valley are few of main valleys in the region. Kashmir Valley is more than 100 kilometres wide and biggest in region. Jhelum, Indus, Tawi, Ravi, and Chenab are major rivers of Jammu and Kashmir. Jammu and Kashmir is also home of many glaciers; the Siachin glacier is seventy-six kilometres long—the longest in region.

The People

According to the 2011 census, Islam is practised by about 68.3 per cent of the state population, 28.4 per cent follow Hinduism, and small minorities follow Sikhism (1.9 per cent), Buddhism (0.9 per cent), and Christianity (0.3 per cent).

Jammu and Kashmir is an abode of multilingual, multireligious different races. Each group has its own distinct and peculiar characteristics of culture, further deepened by geographical divisions created by landscapes, rivers, and mountain ranges. The Jammu region is dominantly Hindu with Muslims being in majority in certain areas. Most of the people speak Dogri. In the mountains, there are three distinct communities with different characteristics of their own, like Gujjars, Bakerwals, and Gaddis, who speak the Pahadi language. The Kashmir Valley presents population with two broad divisions (i.e., Muslims and Kashmiri Pandits, both interestingly speak Kashmiri).

The people of Ladakh are believed to be descendants of a blended race of the Mons of North India, the Dards of Baltistan, and the Mongols of Central Asia. Majority of the population is Buddhist. The Northern area, occupied by Pakistan, is inhabited by different races like Mongols, Tajik, Kirghiz, Uyghur, Yagis, and others. The Muslim population is almost equally divided into three sects (i.e., Sunni, Shia [Jaffaria], and Shia [Ismails]). Pakistan Army sponsored communal violence is very common in POK because of Pakistan's official patronage of the minority, Sunni community. The southern portion of POK, where the majority of people are concentrated (about nineteen lakhs), the common language is Dogri—now dominated by Punjabi.

Division	Population	Percentage
Kashmir	5350811	42.64%
Jammu	6907623	55.05%
Ladakh	290492	2.31%
Total area of three Divisions of Jammu and Kashmir	12548926	100%

Source http://nidm.gov.in/pdf/dp/Jammu.pdf

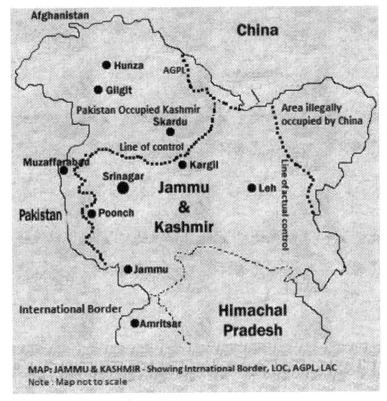

Map of Jammu and Kashmir

CHAPTER 2

LINE OF CONTROL

When Mrs Gandhi, after recounting their points of 1972 Shimla agreement, finally asked Bhutto, 'Is this the understanding on which we will proceed?' He replied, 'Absolutely, aap mujh par bharosa keejiye (you can rely on me).'

---

* P. N. Dhar: Indira Gandhi and Indian Democracy.

CHAPTER 2

Presently, in State of Jammu and Kashmir, Indian Army is holding its position over 1,050 kilometre long stretch, which is divided into international border, LOC and AGPL (Actual Ground Position Line).

As mentioned in previous chapter, India took this matter to UN Security Council, which passed resolution 47 and established the UNCIP to resolve the situation. Ceasefire was called and UNMOGIP (UNITED NATIONS MILITARY OBSERVER GROUP IN INDIA AND PAKISTAN) was established to observe and repost ceasefire violations.

Line of Control

In war of 1971 between India and Pakistan, Pakistan army attempted to alter Cease Fire Line at many places in this region. After ceasefire, to avoid any future attempt of altering it by Pakistan, to counter Pakistan's "Creeping Forward Policy, and to avoid further conflict - a line was agreed as ground position for troops of both sides. A clear map was drafted and signed by top commanders of both sides. This newly drafted line, which is the outcome of 1972 Shimla Agreement is presently known as LOC (LINE OF CONTROL).

Shimla Agreement

Perhaps the most famous meeting between Indian and Pakistani leaders took place in Shimla in 1972 following the Bangladeshi War of Independence. The Shimla Agreement (See Appendix III, Draft of Shimla Agreement) signed by Prime Minister Indira Gandhi and President Zulfikar Ali Bhutto of Pakistan on 2nd July 1972 was much more than a peace treaty seeking to reverse the consequences of the 1971 war (i.e. about withdrawals of troops and an exchange of POWs). The Shimla Accord was intended to lay down the principles of future bilateral relations. It was a blue print for good neighbourly relations between India and Pakistan

The Shimla Agreement contains a set of guiding principles, mutually agreed to by India and Pakistan, which both sides would adhere to while managing relations with each other. These emphasise: respect for each other's territorial integrity and sovereignty; non-interference in each other's internal affairs; respect for each others unity, political independence; sovereign equality; and abjuring hostile propaganda. The following principles of the Agreement are, however, particularly noteworthy:

A mutual commitment to the peaceful resolution of all issues through direct bilateral approaches.

To build the foundations of a cooperative relationship with special focus on people to people contacts.

To uphold the inviolability of the Line of Control in Jammu and Kashmir, which is a most important CBM between India and Pakistan, and a key to durable peace.

India has faithfully observed the Shimla Agreement in the conduct of its relations with Pakistan but Pakistan shamefully always over ruled its own commitments, Pakistan tried to alter LOC many times. In May 1999 Pakistan army's Kargil blunder was a clear violation of Shimla agreement. In paragraph 4 it is very clearly mentioned that "in order to initiate the process of the establishment of durable peace, both the Governments agree that:

Indian and Pakistani forces shall be withdrawn to their side of the international border.

In Jammu and Kashmir, the line of control resulting from the cease-fire of December 17, 1971 shall be respected by both sides without prejudice to the recognized position of either side. Neither side shall seek to alter it unilaterally, irrespective of mutual differences and legal interpretations. Both sides further undertake to refrain from the threat or the use of force in violation of this Line.

Later Pakistan always tries to prove that LOC is not properly marked and uncertain and positions of Indian army posts are vague. It is a big lie told by Pakistan in front of world, as at the time of Shimla agreement LOC was very clearly identified and marked on land as well maps and signed by both officials, Demarcation of LOC took a big exercise and efforts of both side of army leadership and it was very clearly drafted at the time of Shimla Agreement.

As Lt. Gen. M. L. Chibber writes "It is a bit surprising that some people of civil government and army in Pakistan have expressed a doubt that the Line of Control in Kashmir is vague. These statements indicate complete innocence about the meticulous care and thoroughness with which this line was discussed, surveyed where necessary, identified on ground and delineated on maps giving detailed grid references and description of land marks. These were checked and re-checked before representatives of the two countries signed the documents pertaining to this Line and which were thereafter approved by both Governments of India and Pakistan. It is necessary to describe the whole process for those who are not aware of how this crucial matter was handled."

How LOC was Drafted

The representatives of the chiefs of army staff of India and Pakistan (Lt Gen Abdul Hameed Khan of Pakistan Army; and Lt Gen P. S. Bhagat from Indian Army) held a series of meetings alternately at Suchetgarh on the Indian side and Wagah check post on the Pakistan side to delineate the line of control in Jammu and Kashmir, resulting from the ceasefire of 17 December 1971 in accordance with paragraph 4 (ii) of the Shimla Agreement signed between the government of India and the government of Pakistan on 2 July 1972.

A total of nine meetings were held between the senior military commanders of the two countries and their teams between 10 August 1972 and 11 December 1972, alternately at Suchetgarh near Jammu and Wagah near Amritsar. At each meeting, the inputs of sub sectors were discussed, the sticky points resolved, and where necessary, a joint survey was ordered to ensure that nothing was left vague or uncertain.

The line of control was reproduced on two sets of maps prepared by each side, each set consisting of twenty-seven map sheets formed into nineteen mosaics. Each individual mosaic of all four sets of maps, with the line of control marked on them, has been signed by the representatives of the chiefs of army staff of India and Pakistan; and each side has exchanged one set of signed mosaics, as required under the joint statement by the representative of government of India and Pakistan signed at Delhi on 29 August 1972. It is pertinent to add that there were some issues, which had to be resolved by the army chiefs of India and Pakistan; and for these, both the meetings were held at Lahore in November and December 1972 between Field Marshal Sam Manekshaw and General Tikka Khan. All issues were amicably resolved.

The Terrain Along LOC

From Punjab border to Akhnoor town near Jammu, there is clear 199 kilometres of international border, which is clearly mentioned in map and hold clearly by both countries. From Akhnoor to upto point NJ9842, near Turtuk, lies LOC. Beyond NJ9842 lies 110 kilometres of AGPL that divides actual ground position in Siachin between India and Pakistan Army positions.

The international border between Punjab border and Akhnoor is slightly mountainous, but more flat with some rivers crossing across the border, is much more easy for observation than LOC and AGPL. Thus, making it less good and unsupportive for infiltration from outer side. Pakistan always wanted this area to be used as launching pad for infiltrators and smugglers, but failed because of easy to monitor border and lack of any local support.

On other hand, LOC, between Akhnoor and upto NJ9842, is home of few highest mountains, Pir Panjal range, and glaciers.

The major town and villages that lie on LOC are Akhnoor, Naushara, Rajouri, Mendhar, Punch, Uri, Tangdhar, Mushkoh Valley, Drass, Kargil, Batalik, Chorbat La, and Turtuk.

From Akhnoor to Punch, LOC runs along forested mountains and rivers; thus, making it very difficult to trace the crossing of militants in this area. This area is also known as heaven for infiltrators. Same type of culture and habitation across the both sides of LOC in this region make it more difficult to observe cross-border infiltration. Most areas in the region are under developed and with limited resources of road transport and other basic needs. However, Indian Government is trying very hard and approaching for developing and providing basic needs to local people. The situation on other side of LOC (POK) is worst, and people are compromising their lives because of negligence of Pakistan Government in the region. Many villages in this region are located right over the LOC. One more reason makes it worse terrain to secure it from across border terrorism.

Upwards of this region, LOC lies between Pir Panjal and on the great Himalaya range. Punch, Uri, Tangdhar are main towns in this area. Here, mountains are much higher and fully covered with snow in winters and partially in summers. Again, making it more tough terrain to guard. Deployments of forces are less in comparison to lower region of LOC. Here also, villages and habitants on both sides of LOC are quite close to each other. Area is having very less connectivity of roads.

These villagers across the border are used by ISI for running terrorist camps and launching pads for infiltrators to cross the border.

Upwards of this region, LOC runs between great Himalaya range and Ladakh range. Geographically, this region is very different from Uri to Tangdhar region. Here, mountains are much higher with fewer plantations (almost barren) and terrain is much rugged. The area is very less populated. Mushkoh Valley, Kargil, Dras, Batalik, and Chorbat La lies on LOC in this area. Means of transport is very less; the only road that connects this area to Srinagar is NH–1 (Srinager–Kargil–Leh) road. This road remains almost close for half of year. The only connecting road in region makes it more important, and that is why Pakistan wants more dominating position in this area on higher posts along this roadside. This is one of the main reasons why Pakistan invaded higher peaks in region in 1999, which resulted in Kargil War. LOC ends at point NJ9842.

From NJ9842 to Siachin region, Jammu and Kashmir and Pakistan occupied Kashmir is separated by 110 kilometres of AGPL. Siachin is the highest region guarded by forces in the world. This region is almost next to impossible for any type of lifestyle and habitation—a long endless desert of snow.

More significant in today's context is the fact that the LOC represents a broad ethnographic and cultural divide. In present scenario, more or less there are no Kashmiris nor Buddhists nor Dogras nor Kashmiri Pandits on the Pakistan side of the LOC. The people of POK are mostly of the Punjabis, migrated from Punjab region of Pakistan by its army and Hazara-Pathan. In trying to control the area, Pakistan establishment totally destroyed its culture and ethnicity.

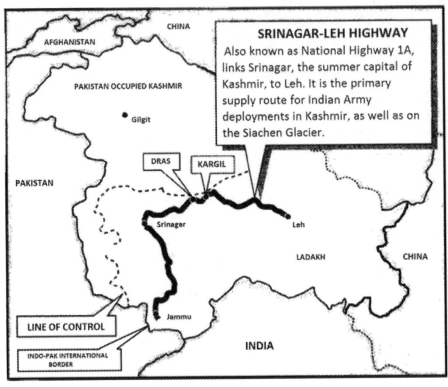

Map Note To Scale

FIG: National Highway – 1A and LOC

REFERENCE

1. MAP: Rahul Bedi, 'India Strikes back at Intruders' Jane's Defence weekly (9, June, 1999) Page no: 6

CHAPTER 3

NUCLEAR TEST AND LAHORE SUMMIT

As long as the world is constituted as it is, every country will have to devise and use the latest devices for its protection. I have no doubt India will develop its scientific researches, and I hope Indian scientists will use the atomic energy for constructive purposes. But if India is threatened, it will inevitably try to defend itself by all means at its disposal.

- JawaharLal Nehru*

---

* In **June 26, 1946, Pandit Jawaharlal Nehru, soon to be India's first Prime Minister, said in a speech at Bombay (Now Mumbai)**

CHAPTER 3

India always believed in 'Atoms for Peace', a non-proliferation program, which aimed to encourage the civil use of nuclear technologies in exchange for assurances that they would not be used for military purposes.

Nuclear Test (Pokhran 2)

This event took place in summers of 1998. On eleventh of May, Prime Minister Atal Behari Vajpayee announced the successful nuclear test conducted at Pokhran in Rajasthan, under code name of 'Operation Shakti'. The test involved five detonations in a series on 11 and 13 May. Prime Minister Atal Behari Vajpayee declared India a full nuclear state.

This was India's second nuclear test. First was Pokhran1 (Operation Smiling Budhha) conducted on 18 May 1974 under leadership of Prime Minister Indira Gandhi.

Pakistan followed the Indian example fifteen days later. That was not a surprise, as its security policy has always been indo-centric, and its nuclear technical capability was known. The government of both countries received massive domestic support after the events, but they faced sharp criticism and all types of sanctions from foreign countries.

The international flak faced by both India and Pakistan, The imposition of sanctions on both countries and Nuclear power capacity of both countries engendered a new sense of responsibility in New Delhi, as well as in Islamabad. Both countries, after nuclear test were in humongous pressure of western countries and UN. Sanctions were imposed, which effected economic reforms very badly, and time has come to act responsibly to maintain a peaceful and tension-less environment for sub continent. Leadership of both countries was sensing the responsibility that the nuclear dimension had added a responsibility to avoid any future conflict between them. To assure the world countries and to normalise the relations between both India and Pakistan, In the next few months, direct and back-door diplomacy between India and Pakistan became hyperactive, which resulted in the Indian Prime Minister Atal Behari Vajpayee's historic bus journey to Lahore, and the signing of the Lahore declaration with Pakistan's Prime Minister Nawaz Sharif on 20–21 February 1999.[1]

Under the international pressure, as well as respecting sentiments of both side of people, the two countries gradually started to ease the tension and seemed to be about to enter a stable and visible nuclear deterrent relationship.

First time after the nuclear test, Prime Minister Nawaj Sharif and Prime Minister Atal Behari Vajpayee met in United Nations General Assembly in New York. Both agreed for meeting, and then met in a relaxed atmosphere on 23 September. Meeting went in very friendly and cordial manner.

After this first meeting of both prime ministers after nuclear test, foreign ministers of both sides started initiating the process of dialogue to ease up the tension in subcontinent and as well to make a platform for state head level talks. The first round of Foreign Ministers talks were held in Islamabad in October 1998. The other six were discussed in New Delhi in November. At the zenith of this process was the Lahore declaration of February 1999.

LAHORE SUMMIT

On 11 February 1999, the Pakistan foreign minister announced the state visit of Indian Prime Minister Vajpayee. On 19 February 1999, Prime Minister Vajpayee was received by Pakistan Prime Minister Nawaz Sharif with a great warm welcome when he arrived by the inaugural bus service from Delhi to Lahore, establishing a new transport link for people of both countries to travel across.

Many of Indian dignitaries, celebrities such as film actors, sport stars, and other noted persons and top journalist were also with prime minister's political and diplomatic delegation.

The two leaders agreed a moratorium on conducting further nuclear test explosions, and pledged a series of confidence-building measures to reduce tension, including a commitment to provide each other with advance notice of ballistic missile flight tests.

The Lahore Summit was regarded as a milestone by both New Delhi and Islamabad because it was the first time since 1972 that the Indian and Pakistani leadership held detailed discussions on their home territories. The outcome of the Lahore Summit was the Lahore Declaration—a treaty agreed and signed by both countries.

LAHORE DECLARATION

The Lahore Declaration (See Appendix-III Lahore Declaration) is a bilateral agreement and government treaty between India and Pakistan. It was signed by Indian Prime Minister Mr. Atal Behari Vajpayee and Pakistan Prime Minister Mr. Nawaz Sharif on 21 February 1999, at the historic summit in Lahore, and given formal consent by the parliaments of both countries in the same year.

The Lahore Declaration was signed along with a joint statement by Prime Ministers of both countries, after three rounds of talks between the leaders of both countries. The Lahore treaty was one of the historic and important treaties between both countries to normalise the relations and ease up the situation after the publicly performed nuclear test carried out by both nations in summers of 1998.

Under the terms of the agreement of Lahore Declaration, both countries agreed to avoid risk of any unauthorised use of nuclear weapons or any nuclear accident. The Lahore Declaration brought responsibility to the leaders of both nations to avoiding nuclear race or any conflicts between countries. This event was significant in the history of India and Pakistan and it provided both countries an environment of mutual confidence.

It was the second nuclear control treaty signed by both countries and assured each other to continue the use of the 1st treaty, NNAA (Non Nuclear Aggression Agreement), which was signed in 1988.

In its content, both governments agreed for their commitment to the vision of peace, stability, development and their full commitment to the Shimla Agreement and the UN Charter.

Both governments recognised through the Lahore Declaration that:

- The nuclear dimensions of the two countries added their responsibility for avoid any convention or non-conventional conflict between them.
- It commits both to the principles and purposes of the Charter of the UN, and the universally accepted fundamental of peaceful neighbourhood.

- It commits both countries to the objectives of universal nuclear non proliferation and disarmament.
- Both governments condemned terrorism and given an assurance of non-interference in each other's internal affairs and to reach objectives of the SAARC and promote human rights in region.
- It reiterated the determination of both countries to implementing the 1972 Simla Agreement in letter and spirit.
- Recalling their agreement of Sep 23, 1998, that the peace and security in region is the first priority for both nations.

Both countries agreed that:

- They will intensify efforts to resolve the Kashmir issue, to resolve disputes between both countries, to enhance bilateral dialogue.
- They will not make any intervention and interference in each other's internal affairs.
- They will intensify their composite and integrated dialogue process.
- They will take immediate steps for reducing the risk of any unauthorised use of nuclear weapons or accident.
- They will take confidence building measures to avoid any conventional or unconventional conflict between both countries.
- They will be committed to the goals and objectives of SAARC.
- They will protect and promote all human rights and fundamental freedoms

Lahore declaration was followed by joint statement of both prime ministers (See Appendix- IV Joint Statement of both Prime Minister) and memorandum of understanding (MOU) between foreign secretary of Indian and Pakistan (See Appendix-V Lahore Declaration).

Reference

1. KARGIL FROM SURPRISE TO VICTORY By GENERAL V.P. MALIK, page no. 27

CHAPTER 4

BACKSTABBING BY PAKISTAN

'Be certain that he who has betrayed the once will betray the again.'

CHAPTER 4

In February 1999, the then Indian PM, A. B. Vajpayee, went to Lahore in a bus with a hope that joint efforts of Sharif and Vajpayee would lay foundation of new Indo-Pak relations. By then, Pakistani troops had captured over 140 posts in Kargil, and our government and army didn't have a clue about it. We were engaged in peace process and were putting our all efforts to improve good relation between both countries; at the same time, Pakistan establishment was planning for its biggest operation after 1971 against India.

On one hand, Pakistan Prime Minister Nawaz Sharif was singing the commitment of keeping peace and harmony between two nations and reiterating the determination of both countries to implementing the Shimla agreement in letter and spirit with the Indian Prime Minister, Atal Behari Vajpyee. On other hand, Pakistan Army, under the leadership of General Pervez Musharraf, was pulling up socks for execution of an already planned operation of altering the LOC and intrusion of Pakistan Army into Indian territory to occupy the strategic heights and areas.

Neither Pakistan Army nor its chief, Pervez Musharraf, were interested in Lahore Summit. Later, he totally rejected the Lahore process, stating it did not address the main issue of Kashmir.

As mentioned by Kargil review committee in its report, RAW shared an input in February 1999 about the monotony and unhappiness of Pakistan Army leadership toward the upcoming event of Lahore Summit. RAW Inputs were:

a) 'The top army brass may not be entirely united in their approach to the proposed thaw in Indo-Pak relations.'

b) 'A section of senior army officers in the GHQ still held the view that Pakistan cannot hope to get a favourable deal from India unless it deals with India from a position of strength.'

These reports were shared with the cabinet secretary, principle secretary to the prime minister, foreign secretary, home secretary, NSC secretariat, and Director of IB.

After a few years, Pervez Musharraf himself proved the inputs right and confessed that he saw Lahore Summit as a waste of time and was never in favour of it.

'I don't see it (Lahore process) as a low or even the high point because, really, the Lahore Summit was not addressing the main issue. It is just a process, which would never have carried forward the dialogue in a concrete manner,' he said in an interview with noted journalist, Mr M. J. Akbar.

He said everyone must realise that the Kashmir problem was the main source of tension between India and Pakistan, for which the two countries had fought wars. 'Anybody who thinks that Pakistan and India can get very chummy, friendly, and cooperate without a solution to the Kashmir issue is not a practical and realistic individual."

Musharraf even suggested to the Pakistan Government to include Kashmir in the final draft of the Lahore Summit. The ultimate draft gave the impression that Kashmir was a minor irritant between the two countries, and there were many other big issues among them.

'I think it should be Kashmir and all other issues, and not all other issues and Kashmir. It ought to be like that if we are realistic and want to improve relations,' Musharraf said in an interview. It clearly shows his disrespect towards decisions, efforts and steps taken by civil establishments of both countries to keep peace and harmony between two countries.

Like most members of the Pakistani military establishment, Musharraf was totally adamant and against normalising the relations with India. One cannot forget that he chose to absent himself from the welcoming ceremony for Vajpayee at Wagah border. It is no secret in Islamabad that he did so because he did not want to be seen saluting the prime minister of a neighbour that he regarded as an 'enemy country'.

It is now very clear that even as the Lahore declaration was being executed between Prime Ministers Atal Behari Vajpayee and Nawaz Sharif, preparations for the intrusions by Pakistani troops were in full swing. This was one more example of Pakistan Army leadership being completely untrustworthy to pursue any peace process between two countries.

Pakistan Prime Minister, Nawaz Sharif, won last election with a commitment of resolving all issues with India by bilateral talks after nuclear test there was huge pressure on both countries to assure peace in region. But on the other hand, Pakistan Army leadership was very much frustrated by the outcome of Kashmir proxy war policy, which was more or less nothing.

There is also a story about protest against Vajpayee's visit to Lahore, which was supported and planned by Pakistan Army establishment.

These protesters belonged to Islamic parties including the influential and ISI favourite, Jamaat-i-Islami, a politico-religious party that called a general strike in Lahore to protest Mr Vajpayee's visit. Carrying banners written 'Vajpayee go home', protesters vowed to keep the Indian leader from setting foot on Pakistani soil.

In Karachi, a cardboard model bus was burnt during another demonstration against Mr Vajpayee. In Lahore, the establishment was unable to manage the crowds mobilised by the Islamists. Vajpayee did visit Minar-e-Pakistan as a grand gesture. But the gesture caused the Jamaat-e-Islami to respond most inelegantly. They washed the Minar to cleanse it of whatever taint may have stuck to it. The evening's banquet hosted for Vajpayee in the Lahore Fort was delayed because mobs obstructed the Indian delegation.

Later, Nawaz Sharif confirmed that, 'It was later revealed to me that the stone pelting on the cars of diplomats and processions against Vajpayee's visit to Lahore in February, 1999 were stage-managed (Pakistan army leadership) and orchestrated by the agencies through a politico-religious party,' Sharif said in an interview to the weekend magazine of *Dawn Daily*.

Moreover, Musharraf is said to have nurtured this idea since 1988 to 1989, and it is claimed that the Pakistani military was engaged in preparations for Kargil even before the two prime ministers met in Lahore. The new-found nuclear status of Pakistan is likely to have fuelled the desire to make sub-conventional gains in Kashmir. Also, string of Siachen is still paining deep inside, and all efforts of taking revenge were badly beaten back by Indian Army. As Benazir Bhutto said in her electronic media interview with journalist, Veer Sanghvi, 'There has always been a plan of Pakistan Army to do some, which could have retrieve us what we lost in Siachan.' She refused the plan when it was put to her by Pakistan Army because she was aware of its bad results and consequences, she said.

According to Brigadier Shauqat Qadir, 'In 1998–99, there was a growing concern in the Pakistan establishment that the Kashmiri cause was losing its international salience and the waning militancy in Jammu and Kashmir needed to be rejuvenated. The military operation, under the garb of a Mujahideen operation, would create a military threat that could be viewed as capable of leading to military solution, so as to force India to the negotiating table from a Pakistan of weakness.'

This made them to plan Operation Bdr. This operation was a part of the Pakistan politico-military strategy with objective of highlighting the Jammu and Kashmir dispute internationally and make diplomatic and military pressure on India. It was also an opportunity to prove his military leadership, as well as tactical and strategic competence to Prime Minister Nawaz Sharif and to the people of his country.

Kargil Review Committee mentioned in its report about Pakistan's strategic motives. Military and Proxy War assumptions are as follows:

<u>**Pakistan's Strategic Motives**</u>

    (a) to internationalise Kashmir as a nuclear flash point requiring urgent third party intervention;

    (b) to alter the Line Of Control (LOC) and disrupt its sanctity by capturing unheld areas in Kargil; and

    (c) to achieve the better bargaining position for a possible trade off against the positions held by India in Siachen.

<u>**Pakistan's Military/Proxy War Related Motives**</u>

    (a) to interdict the Srinagar–Leh road by disrupting vital supplies to Leh;

    (b) to outflank India's defences from the South in the Turtok and Chalunka sectors through unheld areas, thus, rendering its defences untenable in Turtok and Siachen;

    (c) to give a fillip to militancy in J and K by military action designed to weaken the counter-insurgency (CI) grid by drawing away troops

from Valley to Kargil—it would also give a boost to the moral of the
militants in the valley;

(d) to activate militancy in the Kargil and Turtok sectors and open new
routes of infiltration into the Valley; and

(e) to play to the fundamentalist lobby and the Pakistani people by bold
action in Kashmir, which continues to remain a highly emotional
issue.

Pakistan's Assumptions

(a) Its nuclear capability would forestall any major Indian move,
particularly across the international border involving use of India's
larger conventional capabilities. It appears to have persuaded itself
that nuclear deterrence had worked in its favour from the mid-1980s.

(b) Confidence that the international community would intervene at an
early stage, leaving it in possession of at least some of its gains across
the LOC, thereby enabling it to bargain from a position of strength.

(c) China would adopt a favourable posture in the light of its perceived
anti-Indian stand in the post–Pokhran II period.

(d) A weak and unstable government in India would be incapable of a
quick and firm response and would not be inclined to open a new
front.

(e) The Indian Army would not be able to respond adequately due to its
heavy CI commitment in J and K.

(f) Due to an inadequacy of resources east of Zojila, India would not be
able to react effectively against the intrusions before Zojila opened for
traffic by end May/early June.

(g) The Indian Army would not be able to muster adequate forces with
high altitude training and acclimatisation to fight on the Kargil
heights.

(h) Rapidly returning normalcy in J and K needs to be thwarted in order
to sustain its cause.

Operation Planning of Pakistan

Overall planning of Pakistan Army was to make an intrusion under facade
of Kashmir militants into Indian territory to provide a fresh impetus to so
called Jehad in Kashmir Valley. A new attempt to attract focus of international

community on Kashmir issue, and taking a revenge from Indian Army of Siachen through capturing important heights in Mushkoh Valley, Dras sector, Batalik–Yaldor sector by capturing the heights, they can easily dominate NH-1A, which is passing close by these areas. Once they capture and dominate NH-1A, they can easily cut off Siachin from rest of India, and then it can be recaptured easily.

Another military aim was to open up few more infiltration routes for militants, and alter the LOC to null and void the Shimla agreement.

Intrusion took place some time during spring of 1999 (almost same time of Lahore Summit). The preparation was ongoing from 1998. FORCE COMMANDER NORTHERN AREA (FCNA) is a division size formation of the Pakistan Army. It commands the troop deployed in northern areas of Pakistan. It is a component of (X) corps of Pakistan Army. Lt Gen Javed Hassan, a faithful subordinate of Gen Musharraf, was commanding FCNA at that time.

During the winter of '98–'99 between September to March when the entire region was covered under heavy snow and connecting to upper areas is totally closed, Pakistani Army started their execution of Op. Bdr.

According to various theories, the generals planned their misadventure in October–November 1998 when Indian Army started vacating their posts in the beginning of winter. A Pakistani general did recce of the area, and found that there was no army presence for miles. This encouraged them.

As per plan, headquarter 62 infantry brigade was given task by FCNA to execute Op. Bdr. Throughout the winter, troop of NLI, Chitral, Bijaus Scouts, and selected SSG commando were engaged in making extensive preposition of intrusion in Indian Territory. Few artillery units were also bought down from II Corps Peshawar for Kargil adventure.

Later, few Kashmiri militants and Local ISI agent were also involved at the time of war to attract international forum on Kashmir issue.

In the first half of spring, after training for high altitude warfare in the thick of winters, an expected size of 200 infiltrators started their campaign in January. Crawling, they reached Kargil Heights by March and saw scores of Indian bunkers empty. According to various theories, they had planned to capture ten odd posts, but they found them unoccupied, asked for reinforcements, and ended up capturing 140 posts. NLI soldiers spread over entire region of Mushkoh Valley, Dras, Batalik, Tololing, and Kargil area.

Initially, they started patrolling and recce on the ridgeline and peaks, and then started basic infra and supply routes for a number of posts on peaks without showing any presence in a silent way. They quickly built bunkers and sangars, and started deploying heavy weapons including shoulder-fired surface to air missiles and on basic infra and camouflage required. They made an ammunition dumping and stored rations in good quantity, sufficient for them to flight couple of weeks. They made proper reinforcement and supply route in such a good manner that cutting them at the time of capturing peaks was a biggest headache for Indian Army to cut off or destroy them.

The Kargil Review Committee (KRC) analysed and reconstructed Pakistan Army's Op. Bdr. by Pakistani Army personnel's documents, diaries, and radio intercepts captured and recovered by Indian Army and its intelligence agencies.

In above report, the following points came to light:

- In late January, or early February 1999, reconnaissance party/teams of Pakistan Army (which includes officers) crossed LOC.
- In February, this team established a first line of administrative bases, which were very close to LOC, and subsequently more men and support service staff joined.
- These intruders entered Indian side in late April. This was logical as March has heavy snowfall, and early induction would be easily detected and also posed logistics problems to intruders.
- The intruders moved only in gaps between the Indian post, and to avoid more detection by air surveillance i.e., Winter Air surveillance Operations (WASO). Later, they occupied the posts vacated by Indian Army because of winter. In April, they moved further inside 2–3 kilometres and occupied a large area of Indian Territory. The same was also mentioned in one of the recovered document of Pakistan Army in Mushkoh Valley.
- Equipment carried by this team was for snow bound conditions, which included ECC—extreme climate clothing. The even established igloo show tents and sangars using loose rocks.
- These intrusions were got because of these factors:
    o Helicopter vibrations and speed, which did not give a clear observation

o Noise and sound of helicopters gave early warning and ample time to intruders to conceal.

o Limitation of helicopter flight (i.e., it cannot fly after a certain altitude and also the radius of action); distance covered by the helicopter, posed certain restriction in surveillance.

1. Most of the helicopter flights were aimed for detection of militant infiltration, thus, it flew along valley and rivers only which were the main route of militants, not on ridges which were occupied Pakistan Army regulars.

Each ridgeline was held by approximately fifty NLI soldiers under command of a major or captain level officer.

Post were made in such a way that in any case of assault (however they never imagined India will react in such aggressive and intensified way to capture back), another nearby post can give support by corner fire, as well as logistically.

Each post was provided by heavy, light, medium machine gun, rocket launchers, grenade launchers, mortar and craft guns, stringer and artillery support. In easy words, altogether a tough time for Indian Army was waiting ahead.

Pakistan's ORBAT

a) **323 Infantry Brigade (Dansam):** four infantry battalions, seven fire units (each fire unit is an battery consisting of six guns)

b) **62 Infantry Brigade (Skardu):** five infantry battalions, seven fire units

c) **80 Infantry Brigade (Minimarg):** five infantry battalions, eleven fire units, two wings of Chitral Scouts.

d) **Reserve:** one infantry battalions at Gilgit and elements of the Chitral and Bajaur Scouts.

A scrutiny of various intelligence reports, captured documents, prisoner of war (POW), interrogation reports, and signal intelligence also indicates that the intrusion plan envisaged creating four independent groups from four infantry battalions and two companies of special service groups already located on the FCNA region. These were:

(a) 5 Northern Light Infantry (NLI) Battalion located at Hamzigund
(b) 6 NLI Battalion located at Buniyal
(c) 8 and 12 NLI Battalions located at Skardu and Gultari respectively
(d) In addition, some elements of 3, 4, 7, and 11 NLI Battalions were employed for logistic.

A total of eighteen artillery fire units provided fire support to the intruders from the Pakistani side of the LOC opposite the Kargil sector, ensuring that each intrusion area was supported by three to four fire units.
(Source: Kargil Review Committee, From Surprise to Reckoning)

Weapons/Equipment

The weapons/equipment used by the intruders were:

(a) Personal Weapons: G3 rifles and AK 47s
(b) Battalion support weapons: medium machine guns, automatic grenade launchers, RPGs, and 82mm mortars
(c) Air defence weapons: ANZA anti-aircraft missiles, Stinger anti-aircraft missiles, and 12.7mm KPVT
(d) Artillery: 120mm mortars, 105mm mountain guns, and 130mm medium guns
(e) Helicopters: 'Puma' and 'Lama' (MI-17) helicopters
(f) Special equipment: gas masks, passive night vision devices (PNVDs), and snow scooters.

(Source: Kargil Review Committee from Surprise to Reckoning)

CHAPTER 5

A BAD SURPRISE FOR US

'In war, the abnormal is normal and uncertainty is certain.'

CHAPTER 5

If we divide Operation Bdr in two parts: first, to reach the ridgeline and peaks in Indian territory without getting noticed by anyone and take a firm position; second, to hold the position in any case of assault, and don't let Indian soldiers to come up and recapture the posts. Undoubtedly, the first half of Operation Bdr by Pakistan was really an execution of top-class warfare tactics, but second half proved as a biggest disaster for Pakistan, which it ever faced after 1971 Indo-Pak War.

The operation was so secretive that had it been a success; it would have been regarded as great clandestine military operations ever. The intruders, regular army of Pakistan, were firmly holding our peaks for a period of at least three months, hiding themselves from local people, army, and our intelligence agencies. Normally in wintertime, as per tradition, both countries vacate their forward post from peaks because of heavy snow fall and extreme weather. Main reason of doing this was to avoid casualties because of extreme weather and snowfalls. Normally in winters, our units used to focus more over *Nullah's* passing between mountains and areas between ridges on LOC, which were the main routes of infiltration used in winters. But even in winter, there was a normal practise of sending LRPs (Long Range Patrols), which was not properly followed.

As a regular tactics, it is acceptable to vacate the post; but yes, it was a big intelligence failure of our agencies and units, which were deployed and given responsibility of guarding the area. LRPs were not sent, or sent with big gap in time nor any local information was gathered from local peoples.

These are the few main reasons because of which we failed to trace any intrusion on peaks in our territory:

A. **Vacation of Hazardous Posts:** Certain posts, the year-round holding of which could expose troops to the risk of loss of life due to extreme weather conditions and avalanches, are earmarked for vacation. These are called winter-vacated posts, and are vacated before maintenance routes become dangerous.

B. **Winter Cut-Off Posts:** Permanent posts within the various defended areas/locality in which it is operationally necessary to keep under occupation throughout the year, but whose routine maintenance support is not possible during winter months due to snow conditions, are called 'winter cut-off posts'. These posts are stocked up (level of stocking maintained is for 210 days) during the summer months, so that they can sustain themselves without resupplying for the period of they are cut-off.

C. **Reduction in Manpower:** Due to the reduced threat in winter, the reduction in the total number of posts held and reduced patrolling activity, a larger number of personnel are sent on leave and for courses. This reduces manpower availability during winter, as well as the administrative load in these high altitude areas.

During the winters, as soon as movement and patrolling became near impossible due to heavy snow conditions, the additional battalions withdrew from the area. After their withdrawal, no patrolling was carried out in the Mashkoh Valley and Batalik. The period during which patrolling was not carried out in the winter of 1998–99 is as under.

Sector	From	To	Gap
Mashkoh	January 10, 1999	March 30, 1999	80 Days
Yaldor	February 1, 1999	April 5, 1999	64 Days
Kaksar	March 3, 1999	April 11, 1999	38 Days

(Source: Kargil Review Committee from Surprise to Reckoning)

121 (I) Brigade, the brigade responsible for guarding and taking care of any intrusion in area was totally exposed and failed.

We were still in confusion

On 3 May 1998, two shepherd named Tamshi Namgyal and Tsering Morup (residents of Gorkhun Village near Batalik) informed our units the presence of few unidentified people in higher peaks of Batalik carrying guns.

Initially, message was not conveyed properly, or not taken seriously by units and 121 (I) Brigade HQ. No one wanted to believe that peaks were held by Pakistan regular army. Everyone was sure that few handful terrorists were hiding at peaks wanted to come across in Indian Territory.

We sent few patrol parties in forward areas in coming next days on sixth, seventh, and eighth of May. Patrol parties faced heavy fire upon them from peaks. Lt Sourav Kalia of 4th Battalion of Jat Regiment, with a five-member patrol team on 6 May, at Kaksar went missing.

Still units, brigade, div, and command were in a big confusion and did not ring any alarm in hierarchy as well.

On the other hand, artillery fire from Pakistan was getting intensified day by day. Worst setback for Indian Army was on 9 May 1999, shelling of Pakistan Artillery destroyed ammunition dump of 121 brigade.

In fact, four days after Lt Sourav Kalia and party went missing in Kaksar, and a day after the ammunition dump blew up in Kargil, Chief of Army Staff (COAS) General Ved Parkash Malik went to Poland and Czech Republic on a goodwill visit. Not only this. Even as shelling forced residents of Dras, Kargil, and Batalik towns to fly to safer places, the army command of northern command, Lt Gen Hari Mohan Khanna, went on leave.[1]

As Gen V. P. Malik mentioned in his book about the situation, 'On 12 May evening, when I was in Warsaw, Brigadier Ashok Kapur, my military assistant, spoke to the deputy military assistant in New Delhi. He learnt that some militants had infiltrated into the Batalik sector, and that Headquarters 3 Infantry Division was taking action to clear the area. Ashok Kapur conveyed this information to me. Early next morning, before leaving Warsaw for Cracow, I spoke to the DGMO. He informed me that (a) as per Headquarter Northern Command's assessment (till then), about 100 to 150 Jehadi militants appeared to have infiltrated into Kargil, mostly in the Batalik sector. It was localized infiltration. (b) Elements of two units from 3 Infantry Division had been moved to Batalik. (c) Defence Minister George Fernandes, accompanied by the Northern Army Commander and GOC 15 Corps, Lieutenant General Krishan Pal, was visiting Partapur (in the Shyok Valley, Ladakh), Leh, and Kargil on that day. (d) The Vice Chief of Army Staff (VCOAS), Lieutenant Generel Chandra Shekhar, had apprised the Chiefs of Staff Committee (COSC). The Situation, he said, was being handled appropriately at the division and corps level.'[2]

The Kargil review committee, in its report, has identified forty-five important intelligence inputs pertaining to Pakistan activities in the Kargil of these only eleven had filtered through Joint Intelligence Committee and National Security Council. It was observed a big lacuna and lack of togetherness in between all intelligence agencies, and result of it we saw a big dare from Pakistan to occupy our land without much noise and left us in hustles bustle.

The problem as a former special secretary with RAW, V. Balachandran expressed, 'It may not have been as much an absence of intelligence as inadequate strategic assessment to put it simply. Information might have been in bits and pieces, but there was no one to put it together and make sense of the larger picture.'[3]

On 14 May, defence minister, northern army commander, and LOC 15 CORPS, after visiting forward area on LOC, briefed media in Srinagar that the infiltrators would be thrown out in next forty-eight hours.

Forty-eight hours? Is that confidence our defence minister showing in our armed forces, or ill informed? Yes, he was totally ill informed, or we can say informed by the low class of information gathered by our intelligence agencies and three divisions at that time.

Anyways, by the statement of defence minister, it was now confirmed that some arm held group was occupying our forward posts. This statement made a wave of shock in media, as well as each and every person of country. Everyone was in dilemma that how few intruders can capture our forward post and keep dominating us from there. Another big question was that it was never observed that militants ever captured the strategic heights, and keep them holding was of no point to them nor they had much training to hold posts against the any reaction of Indian Army to recapturing them. It was also not helping them in any case as well.

In the continuation of nationwide dilemma, on 19 May, GOC 15 Corps Lt Gen Kishan Pal addressed press conference in Srinagar. He described the situation as a local 'counter-insurgency operation' and declared that the Jehadi militants were backed by Pakistani Army. Pakistan Army is providing them a total support of logistic, as well as ammunition and artillery support. On a question of a media parson that how much time it will take to throw militants out? He replied that it was a 'time consuming operation, and hence no specific time could be given.' (Daily Excelsior, 19 May 1999)

He simply extended the defence minister's forty-eight-hour deadline and left fellow countrymen in a big confusion.

General Malik wrote a factor that contributed the most, to our surprise and to the fog of war, was over inability to identify the intruders for a considerable length of time. Who were they? Where they militants of Pakistan Army regulars? During my telephone conversations from abroad, and during my initial briefing on returning home, I was informed that our intelligence reports and almost all radio intercepts indicated that the intruders were *Jehadi* militants from Pakistan. On the basis of the few visual contacts, they were reported to be wearing black salwars and kameez. The Pakistan DGMO (Lieutenant General Tauqir Zia), in his tele-conversation with our DGMO, continued to deny any knowledge of the ground situation.

Although civil and military intelligence agencies kept reporting that the intruders were *Jehadi* militants from Pakistan, and perhaps a few local militants, our doubts stemmed from the fact that the *Jehadi* militants never defend territories. They never put up a sustained fight from *Sangars* (emplacements made with loose stones) or hold any ground for long. The intensity of the mortar and artillery fire indicated that the Pakistan Army was involved and was closely supporting the intruders. Something we amiss! We, therefore, asked Headquarters Northern Command and 15 Corps to get as much enemy identifications as possible at the earliest.[4]

As mentioned, surprise was a major factor of Pakistan's plan. The initial intrusions were carried out by troops available in FCNA; thus, ensuring that minimum number of troops was inducted for the operations from other areas. Also, employing troops from the local area reduced the acclimatisation period. Battalions from outside of FCNA were moved into the intrusion area as reinforcements at a later stage after the Northern Light Infantry (NLI) Battalions suffered heavy casualties. Further, since artillery build up is a giveaway and a good indicator of an impending operation, Pakistan had cleverly build up adequate artillery over a period of time on the pretext of trans-LC firing. Surprise was also achieved by good radio discipline and use of line communications as far as feasible. When communications were made, these were intercepted by us, but were in several dialects for which we did not have interpreters. [5]

We should be frank in admitting to being surprised (initially) by Pakistan forces in Kargil. The fact that Pakistan intruders surprised us in Kargil is, by now, well established.

DAMAGE CONTROL

By the time it was getting very clear that intruders are not few in numbers and occupying our (including newly made by them) at least 140 posts in our territory at peaks. It was getting very clear that intruders were highly supported with Pakistan regular army. Intruders' action and the way they were responding on our patrol parties and assaults were clearly showing that they were holding very firm positions with high range heavy weapons with a clear sign of holding the posts for a long period.

These immediately following steps were taken by our army to control the damage in month of May:

Batalik sector: 3 PUNJAB launched two patrols on 4 and 6 May to investigate the reported intrusion. The intrusion was confirmed by a 3 Punjab patrol on 7 May. One coy, each of 10 GARH RIF and 16 GREN was immediately moved to contain the intrusion. On 8 May, HQ 70 Infantry Brigade, which was taking over at Dras, was moved and made responsible for the Batalik sector. Soon, thereafter, two BNS (1/11 GR 12 JAKLI), which had just been de-inducted from Siachen and were readily available, were moved on 9 May and were in position in Batalik sector by 10 May.

Dras and Mushkoh sector: Enemy intrusions in the Dras sector were detected on 12 May by a patrol of Ladakh Scouts, and in Mushkoh sector by army aviation helicopters on 14 May. The NAGA Battalion, which had been moved from the valley on 9 May soon after the detection in the Batalik sector, was diverted to Dras and employed from 12 May onwards to intrusion in that area. The 8 SIKH and 28 RR battalions were moved in on 14 May.

Kaksar sector: The enemy intrusion was detected on 14 May by a patrol of 4 JAT in the area of Point 5299 South-West Spur, commonly known as Bajrang Post (the only post vacated by Indian troops on 2 March in the face of extreme snow conditions). Initially, one coy of 28 RR was released to contain the intrusion; and subsequently, on 21 May, 14 JAK RIF moved for deployment in the Kaksar sector.

Subsector Haneef (Turtuk): Seven Pakistani helicopters had been observed flying with underslung loads in the last week of April 1999. A patrol from 12 JAT sent to monitor activity along the LOC was ambushed on 6 May. Subsequent patrol sent on 16 May and 19 May confirmed that the enemy had occupied the ridgeline along and across the LOC at five locations. The 11 RAJ RIF and 9 MAHAR battalions were tasked to occupy defences and the enemy was subsequently evicted by physical assault.

Chorbatla sector: Once the enemy intrusion in Kargil and Haneef sub-sector were established, five Coys of Ladakh Scouts were moved to reinforce the Chorbatla sector. They occupied defences along the LOC during the period 18–31 May, and enemy attempts to intrude into the area.

By 11 May, HQ 15 Corps had assessed that the intrusion had taken place at a number of places in Batalik sector. By 17 May, further evidence indicated that armed intruders had occupied the heights in the unheld gaps between the Indian defended areas in all sub-sectors in various strengths, initially estimated as Batalik (200–500), Kaksar (80–100), Dras (60–80), and Mushkoh (200–500). At this stage, it was not clear whether the intruders were Mujahideens or regulars. It was also a matter of much speculation and confusion as what Pakistan was up to.

Whilst still not clear about the strength and purpose of the intrusion, the urgent steps taken to contain the situation by 15 Corps from the available forces operating in the valley were:

1) 56 Bde to Dras sector by 15 May
2) 79 Bde to Mushkoh sector, 24 May
3) HQ 8 Mountain Division moved to Kargil sector on 29 May, and took over operational control of the Dras-Mushkoh sector by 1 June 1999[6]

a) 3 Infantry Division (1/11 Gorkha rifles and 12 JAK light infantry) deployed in affected area under the command of 70 Infantry Brigade safeguarding Batalik
b) Two battalion from Kashmir Valley (1 Naga and 8 Sikh) deployed under the command of 56 Mountain Brigade[7]

On 21 May, it was confirmed now that intruders were in thousands of number and heavily supported by Pakistan regular army. They were in dominating position and kept a close eye on our activities on highway, roads, and even in smalls track. They were also getting some help from their local agents. Their accurate firing of artillery was conforming that their local agents played their role very intelligently. It was very clear that now we needed to take firm decisions and proper war planning to throw out the intruders from our territory. For next few days, North Block at New Delhi will witness the historic days of Kargil War.

On 24 May 1999, everyone in Cabinet Committee on Security (CCS), the Chiefs Of Staff Committee (COSC), and all other officials dealing directly with the CCS were 'on board'.

As a follow-up to this politico-military strategy, the three chiefs (Indian) had to work out their military strategy and plan of action, which involved the deployment of force in such a manner that we could cross the international border and LOC at a short notice, and thus exercise pressure on Pakistan and prevent its force from focusing only on Kargil. For the military, the immediate tasks ahead were as follows:

- Issue instructions for the mobilisation of forces, ensure preparedness on the mobilisation of forces, and ensure preparedness on the international border/LOC with Pakistan with a view to achieving strategic asymmetry.
- Induct additional troops and resources into Jammu and Kashmir, particularly the Kargil sector, and create a superiority that would enable 15 Corps to get the intrusion vacated.
- Ensure that the additional forces to be deployed on the Pakistan border/LOC were in a state of operational readiness, which would enable them to undertake defensive or offensive operations at short notice.
- Maintain alertness on the border with china.
- Monitor the military situation closely, particularly in 15 Corps. [8]

Indian Army launched its one of the toughest and major operation after 1971 war, 'OPERATION VIJAY'. Air force and naval operations were given the name 'OPERATION SAFED SAGAR' and 'OPERATION TALWAR'. Indian forces are jointly ready now to defend country's pride and sovereignty.

As intruders were in dominating position, the most challenging activity is to move troops in affected areas. They were easily spotting movement of our military vehicle, and suddenly, our vehicles got trapped in heavy artillery, heavy machine gun, and anti-aircraft gun fire.

The only way to move ahead without getting noticed was to move in night and that also without light. Driving heavy army trucks on hill roads is itself a big task, and terrain with damaged roads with a chance of almost hitting a straight bulled was making it more difficult and unachievable, but our drivers done a fabulous job by mobilising our troops and ammunition in affected areas.

We not only reacted very aggressively on LOC by sending our more troops, as well as in other sectors, Punjab, Rajasthan, and Gujarat were given orders to get prepared and ready. Our air force and navy also immediately started its preparation under code name of Operation Safed Sagar and Operation Talvar, respectively.

Pervez Musharraf's assumption, which he later confessed in his book, that India cannot respond to this kind of (*covert*) warfare with a conventional attack on Pakistan army regulars. He also thought that India will not be able to transfer its army units engaged in counter-insurgency in Kashmir Valley; and by the time it will be winter, it would not be possible for Indian Army to make any offence on post holding by Pakistani troops. But he was wrong, our army headquarters and government started to sketch a plan to throw the intruders as soon as possible with full capacity. Indian leadership was in a mood to give Pakistan a strong reaction and a hard time it ever faced since 1971 war. Now, this is Pervez Musharraf and his courtier's time to be surprised.

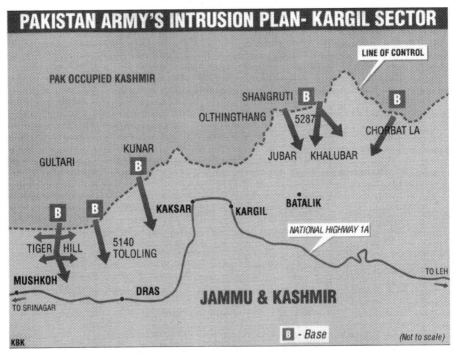

FIG: PAKISTAN ARMY'S INTRUSION PLAN, KARGIL SECTOR

Indian army convoy of trucks delivering supplies to
remote military installations in battle zone.

References

1. Gourav Sawant, Dateline Kargil, page no
2. KARGIL FROM SURPRISE TO VICTORY By GENERAL V. P. MALIK, page no.106
3. Page 91, BLOOD ON SNOW
4. KARGIL FROM SURPRISE TO VICTORY by GENERAL V. P. MALIK, page no.110–111
5. KARGIL TURNING THE TIDE by Lt Gen Mohinder Puri, page no.36–37
6. BLOOD ON THE SNOW By M. G. ASHOK KALYAN VERMA Page No.96
7. BLOOD ON THE SNOW By M. G. ASHOK KALYAN VERMA Page No.96
8. KARGIL FROM SURPRISE TO VICTORY By GENERAL V. P. MALIK Page No.140
9. MAP: Page no 54, Pakistan's Strategic Blunder at Kargil By Gurmeet Kanwal

CHAPTER 6

THE BATTLE ZONE

Even a war zone looks peaceful in most places, most of the time.

- Alex Berenson

CHAPTER 6

Thin air, cold weather, rugged silent mountains half covered with snow make a significant challenge to man's ability to survive at high altitude. This type of terrain is considered very tough for regular mountaineers to climb. Climbing on these mountains with arms, heavy loads of ammunition, reaching the top by ducking oneself from heavy and light gun fire of well-positioned enemy who's sitting comfortably on top, and then make a final assault to capture the enemy post, which most of time was very close gun firing or a hand-to-hand combat. If we look at this terrain, no one can even think of it as a battle zone because of existing extreme weather conditions and heights of peaks. A faint heart is not allowed to even think of combating on these altitudes with these type of condition, but brave-heart Indian armed forces with its sheer will power, who are always known for their 'nothing is impossible in line of duty', once again proved themselves in the conditions where weather is as deadly as bullets and shells of enemy.

Kargil War was fought in Kargil District in the Ladakh division of the state, Jammu and Kashmir. Kargil is situated along the banks of Suru River at an altitude of 2,676 metres. Kargil is located sixty kilometres from Dras town and 205 kilometres from Srinagar City. The population of Kargil is mostly Shia (about 90 percent) and Tibetans as minority.

Most war-affected areas were between the LOC and NH-1A. NH-1A is lifeline of this area, which connect Ladakh district's Kargil and Leh to rest of country. That is why most of intrusions made by Pakistan in this region were to dominate the national high way and cut it off from rest of country. Geographically, the great Himalayan range separates Ladakh from Kashmir Valley. The two other ranges, Zanskar and Karakoram, also pass through this region. The peak in region rises up to altitude of 18000 feet above sea level.

Most of peaks captured by Pakistan Army were between 12,000 feet to 16,000 feet. Most of terrain was made of loose rocks and boulders.

The climate here, even in summer, noted mostly below 0°c. In winter, it goes to -60°c; thus, making its town Dras the second coolest inhabitant in world. Dras was also an area, which witnessed some important battles of Kargil War. Radiation level is 55 per cent higher than sea level, and can cause severe sunburn and snow blindness. Frostbites are very common in this region.

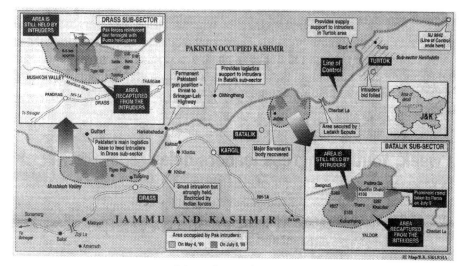

Map of Battel Zone.

The Area of Battles

We can divide area of Kargil War in three main parts of Kargil district.

a) DRAS–KARGIL SECTOR
b) MUSHKOH VALLEY
c) BATALIK–YALDOR SECTOR
d) KAKSAR Sector

a) DRAS–KARGIL SECTOR: In this sector, enemy was capturing Tololing, Point 5140, Area Three Pimple, and line extending toward Point 5353 peaks and Tiger Hill. GULTARI, Pakistan Army, nearest base to LOC was also situated in this region.

b) MUSHKOH–VALLEY: In this region, enemy was occupying Point 4875, Point 4815, and Point 4575 peaks.

c) BATALIK-YALDOR SECTOR: In this region, enemy was capturing Zubar, Khalubar, Kukarthang formation, and Chorbat-LA in Yaldor sector. Pakistan's main supply base Olingathang for its Northern Light Infantry units is in this region, also newly made support base Muntho Dhalo is nearby this area.

d) KAKSAR Sector: Most area of this region is glaciated. The mountains here are more than 15,000 feet. The main ridge is compromising Point 5608, Point 5605, and Point 5280. The only intrusion in area was capturing of Bujrang post (Point 5299) by enemy.

Top view of Indus river and Kargil town valley with Himalayan mountains and blue cloudy sky in background.

CHAPTER 7

LEADERSHIP AND ORBAT

'Leaders do not find fault, they find remedy.'

CHAPTER 7

On 17 April 1999, National Democratic Alliance, a coalition of government led by Prime Minister Atal Behari Vajpayee of Bharatiya Janata Party (BJP) failed to win a confidence vote in the Lok Sabha. New elections were announced to be held on 5 September 1999. Bhartiya Janta Party led caretaker government was functioning, as per our constitution, till new government forms.

Our Civil and Army Leadership at The Time of Kargil War

Mr K R Narayanan (President of India)
Mr Atal Behari Vajpayee (Prime Minister)
Mr Jaswant Singh (Minister of External Affairs)
Mr George Fernandes (Minister of Defence)
Mrs Sonia Gandhi (Chairperson, Indian National Congress)
Dr Manmohan Singh (Leader of Opposition, *Rajya Sabha*)
Mr Sharad Pawar (leader of Opposition, *Lok Sabha*)
Mr Brijesh Mishra (National Security Advisor)
Gen V P Malik (Chief of Army Staff)
ACM A Y Tipnis (Chief of Airforce)
Admiral Sushil Kumar (Chief of Naval Staff)

ORBAT in Kargil War

Northern Command

- XV Corps
- XV Corps Artillery Brigade
- HQ 8th Mountain Division

- 8th Mountain Artillery Brigade (Division Artillery)
- 121 (Independent) Infantry Brigade
- 16 Grenadiers
- 4 Jat
- 3 Punjab
  - 10 Garhwal
  - BSF Bn
  - Detachment 17 Guards (ATGM)
- 56 Mountain Brigade (Matayan)
  - 16 Grenadiers[1]
  - 18 Grenadiers
  - 8 Sikh
  - 1 Naga
  - 2 Rajputana Rifles
  - 18 Garhwal Rifles
  - 13 J and K Rifles
  - 1/3 GR
  - 9 Parachute Commandos
  - Detachment 17 Guards (ATGM)
- (d) • (Independent) Parachute Brigade[2]
  - 6 and 7 Parachute
  - 1 Parachute Commandos
  - Detachment 19 Guards (ATGM)
- 192 Mountain Brigade
  - 18 Grenadiers
  - 8 Sikh
  - 9 Parachute Commandos
  - Detachment 17 Guards (ATGM)
- 79 Mountain Brigade (Dras)
  - 17 Jat
  - 28 Rashtriya Rifles
  - 12 Mahar
  - 13 JK Rifles
  - 2 Naga
  - 9 Parachute Commandos
  - Detachment 17 Guards (ATGM)

- 3rd Infantry Division (Leh)
- 3 Artillery Brigade (Divisional artillery)
- 70 Infantry Brigade (Batalik)
  - 12 J and K Light Infantry
  - 1/11 GR
  - 10 Parachute Commandos
  - 1 Bihar
  - Ladakh Scouts
  - 17 Garhwal Rifles
  - 5 Parachute
  - 14 Sikh
  - Detachment 19 Guards (ATGM)
- 102 (Independent) Infantry Brigade (Shyok River Valley)
- 11 Rajputana Rifles
  - 9 Mahar
  - 13 Kumaon
  - 27 Rajput
  - Detachment High Altitude Warfare School Permanent Cadre
  - Detachment 19 Guards (ATGM)

Kargil Theatre Artillery (these artillery units took part in the war serving under various formations)

Lt = Light; Fd = Field; Med = Medium; Hvy. Mor. = Heavy Mortar

- 4 Fd Regiment
- 15 Fd Regiment
- 41 Fd Regiment
- 108 Med Regiment
- 139 Med Regiment
- 141 Fd Regiment
- 153 Med Regiment
- 158 Med Regiment
- 197 Fd Regiment
- 212 Rocket Regiment
- 244 Hvy. Mor. Regiment
- 253 Med Regiment
- 255 Fd Regiment

- 286 Med Regiment
- 305 Med Regiment
- 307 Med Regiment
- 315 Fd Regiment
- 1861 Lt Regiment
- 1889 Lt Regiment

Other Battalions[2]

- 5 Special Frontier Force (Vikas Force)
- 663 Reconnaissance and Observation Squadron
- 668 Reconnaissance and Observation Squadron
- Ladakh Scouts: Karakoram and India Wings
- 13 Punjab
- 12 Grenadiers
- 22 Grenadiers
- 9 Rashtriya Rifles
- 14 Rashtriya Rifles
- 17 Rashtriya Rifles
- 11 Sikh
- 3 JK Rifles
- 16 Dogras
- Dogra Scouts
- 5 Rajput

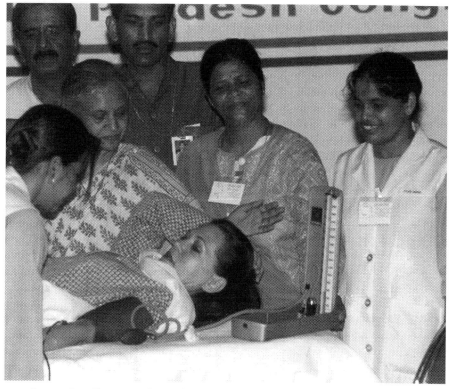

Sonia Gandhi, President of Indian National Congress Sonia Gandhi Donates Blood for The Indian Armed Forces Injured In Kargil Sectore.

Sonia Gandhi, President of Indian National Congress Puts Money Into A Box As She Launches A Three Day Campaign To Collect Donations.

References

1. The reason many infantry battalions are mentioned under different formations is that they fought the war at different times under different brigades.
2. 50th (I) Parachute Brigade were successively army HQ reserve, Northern Command reserve and XV Crops reserve ultimately fighting the war under 8th Mountain Division. They were kept close by for purposes of acclimatisation the contingency plan.

(Source: Indian Army Order of Battle by Richard A. Rinaldi and Ravi Rikhye Page no. 247-248-249)

CHAPTER 8

BATTLE IN KARGIL–DRAS SECTOR

'Veer Bhogya Vasundhara'
('The Brave Shall Inherit the Earth')*

CHAPTER 8

The main intrusions in this area were at feature of Tololing, Point 5140, Tiger hill (Point 4660) and area of Three Pimple. This Kargil–Dras sector was very crucial to us, as well as enemy. The area is very close to NH-1A, and one can dominate the highway easily by seating on nearby peaks. Enemy can also see army headquarters of 56 Brigade. They can easily direct fire on twenty-five kilometre stretch of national highway.

Battle of Tololing

The Battle of Tololing was one of the crucial battles in the Kargil War between India and Pakistan armed forces.

In the early days of May 1999, after patrol parties went missing, in a hustle bustle of recapturing the post as soon as possible, which were occupied by intruders, elements of Northern Light Infantry of Pakistan. 15 Corps decided to deploy 1 NAGA and 18 Grenadiers. 1 NAGA was first to move in battle zone on 11 May, 18 GREN moved on 19 May. No one had clear picture of how many and where exactly intruders were hiding themselves on Tololing, as well as no idea of what type of arms they had?

Tololing is a naked mountain overlooking Dras town from height of 16000 feet. NH-1A, which lies between Dras town and Tololing, was totally exposed, and enemy was dominating the highway with a view of every inch of it very clearly. Accurate attack of shelling by enemy was making it unable for any vehicle movement. This made it more important to get rid of intruders from Tololing to have safe movement of our vehicles, as well as to recover other surrounding posts.

Tololing feature compromises Point 4590, Tololing Top, South-East spur, South-West spur, South spur, Hump on north, and was representative of the deepest penetration made by Pakistan in Dras. One actually has to stand at

Dras and look toward this feature to believe the extent of its domination. From his deployment on the feature, the enemy could dominate the highway both by observation and fire, interdict any move or build-up besides it, cutting off troops along the Bhimbat Valley by direct firing weapons. Hump dominates Point 4590, and Top and Hump was dominated by Point 5140, which supports black tooth. Not only this, but also entrenchment of Pakistani soldiers with bunker fortified with iron girders and corrugated sheets on peaks with clear, long view on steep of mountain was making it worse for Indian soldier to charge offence.

Soldiers needed to climb 16,000 feet within temperature of -10°C with limited winter protection wear because battalions were logistically not prepared for assaults on higher peak, and came straight to battle zone from insurgency effected comparatively lower areas.

As Pakistani soldiers were noticing clearly each and every movement of Indian soldiers, it was very easy for them to aim and shoot the troops, charging uphill inch by inch in daylight. In night, Pakistani fired the flares to light up the surrounding for three to four minutes, an ample time to find troops and shoot them from their safe bunkers.

After three failed assaults of recapturing Tololing on 29 May, the 18th Battalion of the Grenadiers was getting ready to launch an offence to recover Tololing.

In front of their unwavering courage and unstoppable spirit was the challenge of 16,000 feet of steep incline, freezing cold between -5 to -11 degree centigrade, backpacks weighing up to twenty-five kilograms, and choice of more ammunition over food. In addition, climbing up with help of a rope, rifles strapped around their body, moderate clothing with pair of jungle shoes, chilly winds on the way were some of the realities without options. To top it all, Pakistani's advantageous position across Tololing range, supported by bunkers, secured strongly enough to stop our forwarding troops simply by throwing stones and rolling down some boulders, made the target almost impossible to achieve. Despite the strategy to make way from two sides, all efforts of Naga Battalions and Grenadier Regiments could not see much result. In these moments of constant struggle, B Company of 18th Grenadiers, led by Major Rajesh Adhikari, conducted another rather more aggressive assault. In a time when two previous assaults were pushed back with force, this young 28-year-old officer, with his anxiousness, managed to reach beyond the Hump—a point fifteen metres closer to enemy. It was brilliant and daring attempt, but the troop suddenly found themselves surrounded by enemy; and very close, a hand to hand combat was natural outcome of the situation. Major Rajesh Adhikari showed an extraordinary example of courage and bravery, and fought till his last drop of blood. Maj Adhikari, along with Subedar Randhir Singh, Lance Naik RK Yadav, and Grenadier Praveen Kumar gave their supreme sacrifice in line of duty. Another troop led by Captain Sachin Nimbalkar, which was following earlier troops, remained stuck on a cliff behind large rock.

Major Rajesh Singh Adhikari was posthumously awarded the second highest military honour, the 'MAHAVIR CHAKRA' for bravery on the battlefield.

Captain Sachin Nimbalkar took command of assault after Maj Rajesh sacrificed his life.

Then came a bizarre experience for Nimbalkar who led a group of commandos called Ghatak (deadly). Through a crack in a rock, he could see eye to eye and even talk to the enemy. 'Come up, sir, we have no weapons, and you can take your officer's body,' Nimbalkar recalls one of the intruders taunting him to recover Adhikari's body. Nimbalkar cracked then. 'I have come to collect your body as well,' he shouted back in helpless rage.[2]

All the assault were bravely done, but resulted in not much success. Basic reason of failure was lack of intelligent input and logistics. These assault resulted in building up more pressure on 18 Grenadiers, as well as Indian army commanders.

By now, company commander and battalion commanders had realised the dominating positions and very well-armed intruders. But army commanders were in high pressure of Delhi to throw out intruders as soon as possible. As pressure mounted on 18th Grenadiers, reconciling command, Lt Col Vishwanathan, sketched another assault on 2 June. This time, he volunteered himself to lead the assault.

Lt Col Vishwanathan was putting himself for a suicidal mission for the sake of the pride and glory of his regiment. He wrote a letter to his father for not completing his duties for family, but sacrificing his life in line of duty for his nation. He bravely led the assault, but was promptly cut by dominating Pakistan held positions. He gave his supreme sacrifice.

There was a wave of shock in Indian Army. The bodies of Maj Adhikari and his wireless operator were not recovered and were still lying in the battlefield.

Any attempt to recover it was met with UMG fire. Furthermore, the Pakistanis booby-trapped the bodies. One Jawan, who tried to drag Adhikari's body away, lost his hand to a booby trap. Lt Col Vishwanathan's death was taken very seriously by the senior leadership of the Indian Army. Finally, the army was realising the need to get in more firepower before any assault could be made.

The month-long battle was already being likened to the epic battle for the Haji Pir pass in the 1965 war.

Nothing was going in our favour. We were losing our brave soldiers, and moral of our troops was not much high, as they found themselves helpless against the heights and lack of logistic support, and they needed to change their approach toward intruders. They found intruders in more strong position than they thought. Now, our army needed to change its strategy. Senior commanders were very sure that the feature was held by a platoon, at least (approximately forty soldiers) with few of militants and a fire support of six to eight machine guns. They were also well-supported by artillery as well. As intruders had clear view from top, they could bring effective fire on forwarding troops, village, and base as well.

As a writer and researcher on Kargil War, I always found myself puzzled when someone asks me, 'Why our army units never noticed the intrusions in just front of their eyes?' Main reasons I found is senior officers of 121st (I) Infantry Bridge and its unit, 16 GREN 3 JAT, 8 BSF, 4 GARWAL, who were responsible for defence of these areas, senior official showed some lack of accountability and professionalism while performing their duties.

On first of June, Headquarters 8 Mountain Division under Major General Mohinder Puri took command of Dras sector. A decision was taken also to engage more artillery in battle to soften the target. The decision of fresh troops to be engaged was also taken as 18 GREN suffered casualties, and were restless for last twenty-one continuous days.

The 2 Raj Rif, a battalion famous for enviable record of bravery, was immediately ordered to complete the remaining task of 18 GREN to capture Tololing.

For the next nine days, army moved more than twenty batteries, each had six howitzer boffors and medium-sized guns. 2 RAJ RIF started their preparations as well.

2 RAJ RIF, commanded by Lieutenant Colonel (Lt Col) M. B. Ravindranath, prepared his unit for ground combat at high altitude and won

a series of impressive victories. 2 RAJ RIF deployed to Sonamarg from Kashmir Valley where it was conducting CI operations. The battalion remained in Sonmarg for a few days before departing for the combat zone in Dras. At Sonmarg, Lt Col Ravindranath initiated planning, forming teams of senior leaders charged with creating a mountain assault doctrine, an acclimatisation program and a logistic support plan. These efforts proved to be the determining factor in the battalion's success. The battalion requisitioned large quantities of cold weather gear, and minimised soldiers' load to a light assault kit during the attack. The acclimatisation program, cut short to eight days from the army standard of twelve, resulted in no high altitude illnesses in the troops of battalion at the time of assalt. Colonel Ravindranath's preparation was showing his positive approach to high altitude warfare tactics, which would be tested on Tololing very soon.

Meanwhile, the hard lessons learned from 18 GREN were being absorbed by 2 RAJ RIF. They conducted mock operation as well. Colonel Ravindranath was working very hard on maps and chalked out their assaults strategies.

The weapons and ammunition were test fired, an exercise that eliminated a defective lot of hand grenades the soldiers were issued with (army sources later clarified that this can happen sometimes when ammunition are stored for long periods). Heavy ammunition was physically carried up the slopes below Tololing by the washer men, cobblers, and barbers of the battalion—it took four people to support one soldier in this battlefield. 'We were primed for the attack,' said Lt Parveen Tomar, 23, commissioned just five months ago, known as the baby of the battalion.[3]

Finally, the D-day has come, 2 RAJ RIF to launch an attack on Tololing by 1800 hour, and 18 GARH RIF to launch an assault on point 5140 at 1900 hour of same evening.

An entire artillery brigade opened fire simultaneously. All the 120 guns were firing at Tololing peak and all directly. For the first time, howitzers (Bofors guns) were put in the direct firing mode (It fired direct on targets through a low trajectory). The barrel of the 155 mm howitzer pointed at the bunkers on the peak and the guns fired non-stop. The artillery attack began with the Bofors followed by a non-stop firing of MBRLs.

After almost six hours of continuous artillery firing, enemy was badly shaken but was still holding safe in well-built bunkers. The idea of artillery was perfect; accuracy of fire gave Indian troops an advantage to accelerate themselves toward the top. As one of intercepted wireless message of enemy in which they reported, *'Janab lag raha hai jaise aasman gir gaya hai hum par'* (Sir, looks like the sky is falling over us).

CO ordered to line up his four companies: Alpha, Bravo, Charlie, and Delta. He himself handpicked the best soldiers of his unit for the said four assault teams. He started the final pep talk to his men. He explained their glorious history of Rajputana Rifle Regiment, and asked them to give their complete dedication to successful completion of their assigned tasks. He said, 'I have given you what you wanted. Now, you have to give me what I want.' All of sudden, 'Sir, come to the Tololing tomorrow morning, we will meet and have tea with you there,' JCO Bhanwer Singh said very confidently to his CO with a battle cry of 'Ram Chandra ki jai', the assault has started now.

Company Charlie *C* and Delta *D*, led by Major Vivek Gupta and Major Mohit Saxena, set out for assault; and company Alfa *A* and Bravo *B* were nominated reserves of attack. Company *C* and *D* moved quickly on the both axis and advances. By the support fire, one team charged up, and another went around lower to cut supply chain of Pakistanis. The team led by Maj Gupta launched its attack from backside of post and almost reached on the top. Maj Gupta fought bravely and showed a great capability of leadership. He was also lucky to have a soldier like Digander Kumar in his platoon. Digendra Kumar showed a great example of bravery in capturing bunkers by hurling a number of hand grenades in bunker, as well as in hand to hand combat in a very close battle. He overcome enemy and captured the bunkers of Tololing. Despite suffering so many bullet injury, brave Maj Vivek Gupta continued to lead his men to evict the last enemy from top and catching the flying enemy by gun. He fought till his last drop of blood. Maj Vivek Gupta, son of an air force officer and husband of an army officer, gave his supreme sacrifice in his line of duty.

Tololing was captured, but enemy was in no mood of leaving it, as loosing Tololing was big setback for enemy. Enemy launched counter-attacks at that time a young artillery forward observation officer (FOO), Captain Mridul Kumar Singh, took command of *C* company and fought and led the assault very bravely against enemy, and didn't let the enemy recapture the post by beating one by one three counter-attack.

2 RAJ RIF then launched *A* company under Major Padampani Acharya to capture rest of point 4590, and *B* company was tasked to secure northern flanks of Tololing.

Finally, we captured the Tololing, a battle which proved to be a turning point of the Kargil War. The brave JCO, who invited CO Ravindra Nath to Tololing for a tea in morning, was no more, but Tololing once again belonged to India now.

In this hard-fought, crucial battle, Captain Vijyant Thaper, Subedar Bhanwer Lal, Company Havildar Major Yashvir Singh, Havildar Sultan Singh, and Naik Digendra Kumar displayed inspiring bravery. A major contribution was made by Captain N. Kengurese who, with the commando platoon, has been tasked to establish a block between Hump (a feature with about ten high grounds on the same ridgeline about 500–700 metres north of Point 4590) and Tololing. Lieutenant Colonel Ravindernath exhibited dedicated and distinguished leadership qualities.[4]

Major Vivek Gupta was awarded by Mahavir Chakra (Posthumously) for his extraordinary bravery and leadership. Nayak Digendra Kumar was also awarded by Maha Vir Chakra.

After successful capturing of Tololing and Hump, preparation of capturing of Point 5140 were ongoing. The task given to 13 JK RIF to capture it on 18 June after almost first success of 2 RAJ RIF, assault begun.

On 16 June, 13 JK RIF launch its one company to capture rocky KNOB. They were able to capture it soon without much protest.

On 17 June, 13 JK RIF took over whole Tololing ridge as 18 GREN and 2 RAJ RIF being relieved for rest and recreation.

While the attack on Tololing was a super success, the attack on Point 5140 did not meet with any success.

Battle of Point 5140

On 18 June, a brigade level assault was planned to recapture the Point 5140. Considering the large size of objective, a multidirectional assault was planned. 18 GARHWAL RIF from east, 1 NAGA from south-west, and 13 JAK RIF from south were given the task to assault. The entire formation and other adjacent formation were heavily fired for surprise attack of 13 JAKRIF from south slope.

B and *D* company led by Cpt Jamwal and Cpt Vikram Batra were ready to assault and started climbing very silently—idea was to catch enemy by surprise without getting noticed. Initial plan was to get as much as near to enemy post and capture it.

In normal battle exercises, the artillery stops firing when the infantry soldiers are 400 metres from the target in order to prevent any accidental injury to own troops by own fire. But this was no battle exercise. The artillery commanders has been ordered to stop firing when the soldiers were 200 metres from the target. Undetected, the two companies, covering either flank, managed to climb up 200 metres from their target without being detected. The artillery fire was so strong that the enemy troops did not dare raise their heads and hid in their bunkers. Batra and Jamwal informed the base that they were 200 metres from the target, and immediately on the wireless, orders were passed for the artillery to stop firing.

But moments after the artillery guns, including the MBRLs and 105 mm guns, stopped firing, the enemy soldiers came out of their bunkers and opened fire on the advancing Indian troops. Batra and Jamwal realised that there was no way they could climb in the face of such an intense carpet-firing by the enemy machine gunners. And the two youngsters (Batra was twenty-four and Jamwal twenty-five) had decided they would not let their men walk into the jaws of death if avoidable. They radioed back to the base asking for more artillery fire till they reached 100 metres from their target. The commanders at the base were foxed, even worried; but then in war, both Batra and Jamwal were the commanders and the final decision lay with them because they were leading the assault.[5]

Capt Batra and Capt Jamwal advanced with their troops as much as near the Pak bunkers, and then start lobbing hand grenades in bunkers—one by one in seven bunkers. Almost at same time, both informed their CO with famous code message of victory, 'Yeh dil mange more' (Capt Vikram Batra) and 'O yes ya ya' (Capt Jamwal)

A cheer went up at the brigade headquarters. Peak 5140 had been taken. Pakistani forces had been pushed back even further. 'How about the casualties?' the commander asked. There was not a single casualty. 'Not a single soldier died in the operation,' Joshi said.

The victory of Peak 5140 again would make to textbooks on mountain warfare for the manner in which the operation was executed. This was a brilliant operation where a peak at 17,000 feet was snatched from the jaws of a powerful enemy without a single soldier losing his life. This was the perfect execution of an operation by the JAK RIF.

In continues of assaults made at nearby features of Tololing, formations Black tooth, Area Rocky, Rocky Knob, Point 4700 were captured by 1 NAGA, 18 GARHWAL RIF.

Battle of Area Three Pimple

Three Pimples is a cluster of sharp, imposing mountaintops. This area is located near point 5,100 on the Marpola ridgeline, west of Tololing Nala. The Three Pimples complex consists of three: Knoll, Lone Hill, and Three Pimples. This complex dominates the national highway, Dras Village, and Sando Nala. From here, the enemy could observe the movement of troops and armaments and subject them to artillery fire. Close reconnaissance by two Rajputana rifles revealed that Three Pimples, and Point 4700 were well held with at least six sangars in place. The task to capture Three Pimples was given to this same battalion, which has broken the stalemate at Tololing.[6]

On 27 July, the D-day and 1700 the H-hour decided. About twenty artillery fire units (120 guns, mortars, and MBRL) were opened for a hailstorm of TNT on enemy posts. Some of Bofors engaged in direct firing.

D company led by Maj Padampani Acharya and *A* company led by Maj Mohit Saxena, heroes of first Indian victory of Tololing, went in for assault. Attack was almost faltered at the very beginning when the frustrated enemy opened heavy artillery fire on the leading platoon, inflicting large numbers of casualties. Unmindful of the hail of bullets from the enemy's position, Major Acharya crawled up to the enemy position and lobbed grenades. *A* company held their position and soon, *D* company linked up with them at KNOLL formation. Now, 'THREE PIMPLE' was next target.

Mohit Saxena, who had displayed outstanding courage in the battle of Tololing, once again managed to lead his company through a treacherous route without getting noticed. He assaulted the enemy position from the south. To accomplish this feat, he had to climb a sheer rock face over 200 feet high. His daring leadership enabled his men to capture Lone Hill. Along with him, rifleman, Jai Ram Singh, of the assault platoon also displayed extraordinary bravery and camaraderie with this officer. *D* company was assisted in this battle by Captain N. Kenguruse, the commando platoon commander. Without any special mountaineering equipment, he scaled a sheer rock face barefooted, literally hanging on by his fingers and toes. After reaching the top, this fearless officer killed two enemy soldiers who were manning a universal machine gun; and later, another two with his commando knife, before he was fatally wounded.[7]

On other hand, Major Padampani Acharya, in this daring assault, was seriously injured. Despite heavy injuries and unable to move, he ordered his men to leave him and charge at the enemy while he continued to fire. Capt Vijyant Thaper volunteered himself and led assault. He went crazy, his gun was blazing and literally signing death statements of enemy. He gave the enemy a major setback before getting hit by a bullet. The enemy position was finally overrun and the objective was captured. The whole nearby formation was captured by Indian Army by 29 June. Major P. Aacharya and Captain N. Kenguruse were posthumously awarded MAHAVAIR CHKARA by government of India. Captain Vijyant Thaper was awarded Vir Chakra.

2 RAJ RIF, commanded by Lt Col M. B. Ravindranath (he was promoted to Colonel during the Kargil War) showed great examples of a unit that made right adjustments, and whose victory provided a turning point in conflict. CO Ravindranath was awarded for his extraordinary example of war planning, and for motivating and leading his troops and giving Indian Army much needed edge in war.

Tiger Hill

Indian Army got success in Batalik sector and Tololing. It almost changed the table. By the beginning of July, we were dominating more positions than enemy no; but still, Tiger Hill was standing tall right on NH-1A under occupancy of enemy.

Tiger Hill is biggest mountain feature in the region rising to almost 5,090 metres. Located ten kilometres toward the LOC from Srinagar-Kargil-Leh. It gives a clear, long view of highway to enemy sitting on it; thus, it was very important for Indian Army to evict enemy from it.

Pakistan was holding Tiger Hill very well. A company above was deployed to hold it and keep dominating the highway and movement from there. Topography of Tiger Hill was also giving an edge to enemy over our Indian Army.

Tiger Hill features 2,200 metres from west to east and 1,000 metres from north to south. From 500 metres west of Tiger Hill is a smaller feature named India gate and more 300 metres away feature Helmet is situated. This feature was guarded very strongly, which was giving Tiger Hill a fort-like look.

Media persons had already access to Dras region at the time of battle. They presented it as impossible to capture and made it a biggest challenge for nation to recapture it. Tiger Hill assault was captured by media right from the ground zero, and was telecasted almost live.

The task of capturing of Tiger Hill was given to 192 Mountain Brigade. 192 Mountain Brigade was led by M. P. S. Bajwa. A brigade level assault was planned. 192 Mountain Brigade gave the opportunity to 18th GREN and 8th Sikh to recapture it.

Both units examined the feature very closely and pen down the possible routes of attacks and enemy supply chain. The tactic we used in capturing Tololing emerged as best concept to capture Tiger Hill. Now, same type of tactical plans, employment of artillery and air support was needed to recapture Tiger Hill. As the war progressed, Indian commanders were mastering this concept of assault very beautifully.

As I mentioned, 18 GREN and 8th Sikh were given the task of capturing the Tiger Hill by 192 Mountain Brigade.

C company and 'GHATAK COMMANDO' platoon of 18 GREN was led by a dynamic young man, Lt Balwan Singh, age of twenty-two. They start assault from northern flank of Tiger Hill. Lt Sachin Nimbalkar of 18 GREN with his *D* company, leading the assault from eastern flank.

As it was a multidirectional assault, Maj Ravindra Singh and Lt Sherawat of 8 Sikh were leading the assault with their 4 JCO and fifty-two soldiers from front side of Tiger Hill.

On evening of 3 July, artillery was ready to start the battle of recapturing the Tiger Hill with its 120 field and medium guns and 122 mm multi-barrelled Grad rocket launchers. Air force also targeted Tiger Hill on second and morning of the third of July, and hit the bull's eye many times.

The day progressed as usual. Probably, the Pakistani observation post officer spotted nothing different this morning, as everything remained quiet till afternoon.

On this day, the weather was in our favour. There was no moonlight, completely dark, and clouds and drizzle were making it more difficult to spot any movement of our troops for the enemy sitting on top, but the enemy was in far better situation by sitting on top of us.

Artillery started its first fire at 1700 hours, and then altogether started firing at top and other enemy occupied feature of Tiger Hill and it was like a Diwali (Indian festival of lights) when all Bofors fired together.

The infantry assault begins. Tiger Hill was very well-defended by Pakistan from three sides like a fort. The fourth side was sheer drop of thousand feet, and there it was, not well defended. Enemy thought it would be impossible to climb from there, but they never thought that Indian troops were ready for each and every impossible move to recapture Tiger Hill.

After a silent prayer, 18 GREN and 8th Sikh started advancing on the feature. The whole assault depended on perfect coordination of both units. In case 8th Sikh fails, 18 GREN were to be trapped to death; and if 18 GREN failed, their sacrifice and life of 8th Sikh would be a waste.

Intense fire of Bofors was keeping the head of enemy down, and giving a good opportunity to Lt Balwan, Lt Sachin, and their team to move up to Tiger Hill as much near to the top. 8 SIKH also started their operation.

Usually after a spell of five to six hours, artillery fire stops, so our troops started climbing over the feature to capture the target. But this gives enemy a chance to monitor our movement and their aim by sitting on top. So there was some change in plan, usually safe distance for artillery fire is considered around 400 metres, so that its splinters can't harm you. But in this assault, it was planned that our artillery will not be stopped till 200 metres from target.

Tiger Hill had to be taken at all costs. The artillery usually stops firing at the target when the infantry soldiers are 400 metres from the target. This is because the splinters fly up to 400 metres. But in Tiger Hills, we told our infantry troops that we would continue firing till they are 100 metres from the target. Our brave soldiers knew they may die by our firing too. But there was no alternative.

Lt Sherawat started climbing from front as per the plan. Enemy's post started heavy firing on them. Lt Sherawat and his men were giving enemy a tough time. They were sending bunker and machine gun location of enemy to base for exact artillery fire. They knew that they can die by their own artillery, but there was no other alternative. As enemy fire was getting more intense, Lt Sherawat sought for reinforcement immediately. Major Parmar joined the assault. They were turning each and every stone to get an upper hand on enemy. At this point, they got to know that the enemy found themselves trapped and sought for reinforcement to secure the flank, a good sign for our assaulting troops.

On other hand, Nimbalkar and Balwan, with their men trying to nuke foothold on the sheer rock face, the side from where enemy never though Indian Army can make an assault.

Lt Balwan was fortunate that he was leading the synonyms of courage and bravery named Grenadier Yogendra Singh Yadav in his platoon. Yadav himself volunteered to lead the assault and fix the rope for rest of his team. Their immediate task was to reach the top and destroy the enemy bunker, so that Captain Nimbalker and team can process to final assault.

Both teams were climbing independently, but depending on each other to move further. At that moment, enemy got a sniff of our advancing troops and started firing light fires. It gave enemy a clear view of our troops, and they opened machine gun fire. Balwan was totally exposed and got hit. A wave of shock ran through platoon by seeing their commander hit by bullets.

Now, this was the time when Grenadier Yogendra Singh Yadav realised the situation, and led the assault from front demonstrating great courage and bravery. As General V. P. Malik mentioned in his book about Grenadier Yogendra Singh Yadav, 'He was part of the leading team of the Ghatak (commando) Platoon tasked to capture Tiger Hill top on the night of 3/4 July 1999. This approach to the top, at a height of 16,500 feet, was steep, snow-bound, and rocky.' He volunteered to lead the assault and fix a rope for the rest of his team to follow.

The Ghataks succeeded in surprising the enemy. On seeing his team reach the top, the enemy reacted violently and opened up intense automatic machine gun, grenade, and rocket fire, killing Yogendra Singh Yadav's team commander and two colleagues. The further advance of the platoon was stalled. Realising the gravity of the situation, Yogendra Singh Yadav crawled up to the enemy position to silence it, and sustained multiple bullet injuries. Disregarding his injuries and braving the thick volley of enemy bullets, he continued toward the enemy's *sangar* and lobbed grenades inside, all the while firing from his rifle. He killed four Pakistani soldiers in close combat and silenced the automatic fire. In this action, and while repulsing a counter-attack, Grenadier Yadav was hit in his left arm and right leg. Undeterred, he crawled forward to destroy yet another *sangar*. Inspired by this fearless daredevilry, the rest of the Ghatak Platoon fell upon the enemy's position with vengeance and succeeded in capturing Tiger Hill's top, a high priority objective. For most conspicuous courage, well beyond the call of duty, Grenadier Yadav was decorated with the Param Vir Chakra, the nation's highest gallantry award.[8]

Enemy could not believe that Indian soldier could come all the way here from this side of feature.

The Sikhs, on the other hand, were battling the whole night with enemy on front side of mountain. They were confusing enemy by shouting 'Jo Bole So Nihal' on megaphone. This tactics confused enemy that it was a brigade level attack from front side of mountain. Enemy was caught on wireless trying to pass the message of reinforcement and artillery fire on Indian troops in a hustle bustle.

The Sikhs had been directed to ensure that the Pakistani soldiers had to be engaged as long as possible. And this they did throughout the night. Launching deception attacks in different places, engaging the Pakistani soldiers in skirmishes, leaving the top to be taken by the grenadiers. It was only when the grenadiers launched an assault to take Tiger top that the Pakistani realised that the side-spur skirmishes were only a deception. But by that time, it was too late for them to start climbing again to the peak. The Sikhs had gained an upper hand in two flanks, and were steadily climbing to reinforce the grenadiers if required.[9]

Now, our troops were in a dominating position at feature and ready to launch final assault on the top from all sides. But still, there was a big problem in between the victory and the open supply line of enemy. Enemy was easily able to reinforce the top by sending more troops, as well as ammunition. By realising the situation, commanders at base decided to launch assault at point Helmet and Point India Gate (both located on western spur). This move was very essential to cut supply chain of enemy.

The western spur of Tiger Hill extended up to 1.5 kilometres. The approach to the spur where 8 Sikh was deployed was along a steep rock face. A column of 8 Sikh led by Major Ravindra Singh and Lieutenant R. K. Sehrawat, comprising four JCOs and fifty-two soldiers, climbed this rock face under poor visibility conditions and was able to capture India Gate after a tough fight. In this battle, Subedar Nirmal Singh led the assault platoon. He was engaged in hand-to-hand fighting till the end, and was also responsible for beating back an enemy counter-attack.

Despite heavy casualties, 8 Sikh exploited its success up to Helmet and captured this objective on 5 July.

The enemy launched two counter-attacks with forty to fifty personnel, but 8 Sikh fought gallantly and was able to repulse them. Naib Subedar Karnail Singh and rifleman, Satpal Singh, who were part of a platoon deployed on the reverse slope of Helmet, showed exceptional courage. In one of these counter-attacks, Captain Karnal Sher Khan of the Pakistan Army was killed. His body was subsequently handed over to the Pakistani authorities. Other bodies of the Pakistani soldiers found scattered around the battleground were collected and buried appropriately.[10]

On 8 July, entire Tiger Hill was recapture, 18 Grainder hoisted the Indian tricolour on the hilltop. Town Dras and NH-1A in this region were finally safe now.

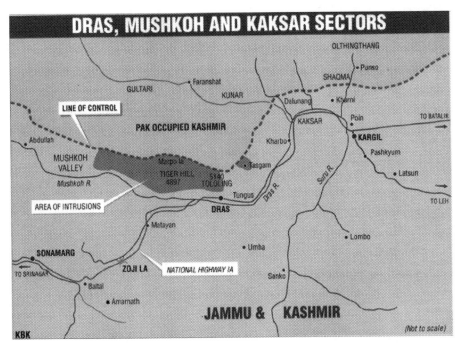

FIG: DRAS, MUSHKOH AND KAKSAR SECTORS

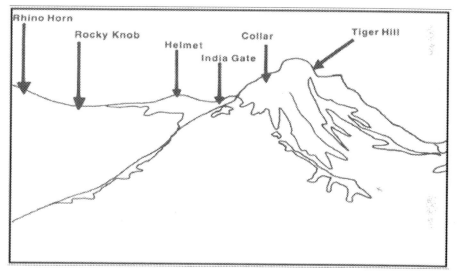

FIG: TIGER HIL

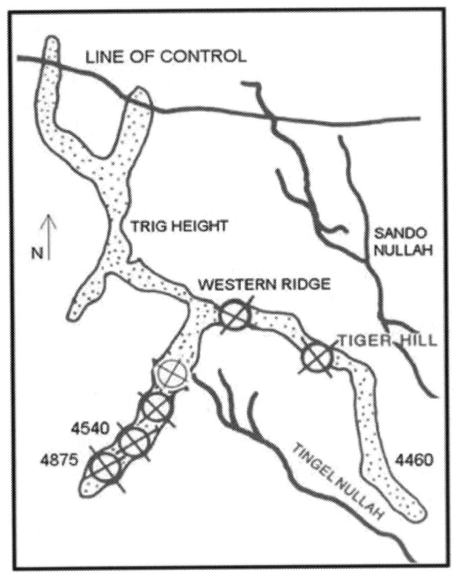

FIG: OVER HEAD VIEW OF ENEMY POSITION
ON TIGER HILL AND NEAR BY POST

Captain Jayashree Salutes June 16, 1999 In New Delhi To The Body of Her Husband Major Vivek Gupta.

References

1. A Ridge Too Far: The Battle For Tololing, L. N. Subramanian
2. India Today, Ramesh Vinayak, addition 5 July 1999
3. Ramesh Vinayak, India Today
4. Kargil from surprise to victory, Gen V. P. Malik Page No. 162
5. Kargil from surprise to victory, Gen V. P. Malik Page No. 162
6. Kargil from surprise to victory, Gen V. P. Malik Page No. 162
7. Kargil from surprise to victory, Gen V. P. Malik Page No. 169
8. Kargil from surprise to victory, Gen V. P. Malik page no. 172
9. Dateline Kargil, Gourav Sawant, page no. 129
10. Kargil from surprise to victory, Gen V. P. Malik, page no.174
11. MAP: Page No. 57, Pakistan's strategic Blunder at Kargil by Gurmeet Kanwal
12. MAP: Page No. 117, The Kargil War by Ashok Krishna Major Gen. Indian Army (Retired)
13. MAP: Page No. 39, High Altitude Warfare: The Kargil by Marcus P. Acosta, June 2003

CHAPTER 9

BATALIK BATTLES

'Why do you want to join the Army?'

'I want the Param Vir Chakra.'

(Param Vir Chakra awardee, Lt Manoj Pandey, replied to interviewer in his Service Selection Board (SSB) interview few years back before Kargil War.)

CHAPTER 9

During the Kargil War, Indian Army faced the toughest challenges in Batalik area. Batalik comes under district Kargil. It was the main region where Kargil war was fought. Batalik can be reached by roadsides, Srinagar, and as well as Leh. Batalik is fifty-six kilometres from Kargil and approximately 250 kilometres from Srinagar. Dah, Garkhan, Hanu, and Darchak are main villages in area. The local resident of these areas are Drokpa Tribe, and believed to be ancestors of Alexander's army and famous as original and pure 'Aryan' breed. Batalik sector mostly lies between LOC and Indus River. It is the highest battlefield in the world after Siachin at the height up to 16,000 feet.

On 3 May, this was the area where very first local shepherds reported the intrusions of enemy in our area at heights.

In the Batalik sector, the LOC cuts across the Indus River between Batalik and Yaldor, and then runs roughly along the Shangruti and Chorbat La watershed on the Ladakh Range at heights that are well above 16,000 feet. Thereafter, the LOC dips a bit toward sub-sector, Haneef (SSH), south of the Shoyk River. Troops of 5 Northern Light Infantry (Pakistan) had intruded 8-10 kilometres in the unheld areas, lying to the west of Chorbat La. They had occupied four of ridgelines, which jut southwards like the fingers of a hand from the knuckle along Chorbat La watershed. These ridgelines, Jubar, Kukarthang, Khalubar, and Point 5203 Churubar Point, vary in height from 15,000 feet to 16,800 feet. Here, 70 Infantry Brigade, under Brigadier Devinder Singh, had arrived just in time to ensure that the enemy did not extend the intrusion to dominate the Leh-Batalik-Kargil road.[1]

Main intrusions made by Pakistan in this region were Jubar Complex Point 5203, Point 4812, Kukarthang, Khalubar, Turtuk, and Chorbat LA.

Most dominated holding of Pakistan was Jubar Complex and Khalubar Peak. It is very difficult to climb these knife-edged peaks, the lowest of which are more than 16,000 feet high.

Our intelligence inputs and pictures taken by our air force showed there were some six to seven hundred intruders on the heights. The second problem with the peaks here is that they gently slope into Pakistan. So the intruders keep climbing till they reach the top, which is in India. We can imagine the strength in this region by the fact that they had set up an administrative base and logistic support base in Munth-Dhola and Sangruti. Their supply chain was so strong that they had a helicopter base, as well as snow scooters were being used for mobilisation; small telecommunication base was set by laying telephone line from administration base to captured area for better connectivity. There were also small medical rooms created to support injured troops. Only in Khalubar were there more than ten to eleven bunker, having two machine guns in each (mostly one bunker had one machine gun). Jubar, Kukarthang, and Khalubar Top were occupied by more than 1,000 soldiers of 5 and 8 NLI. Even in this dominating position, Pakistan suffered most casualties.

The bulk of casualties, almost seventy-two, have been listed as occurred in the Batalik sector that saw some of the most aggressive battles during the conflict. In its official records, the Indian Army has listed that ninety-nine bodies of Pakistani soldiers were recovered in Batalik, and most were buried in Indian Territory. Indian records say a total of 249 bodies of Pakistani soldiers were recovered during the battle, estimation of total enemy casualties was around 1,000–1,200, which was later confessed by the Pakistan Army and civil authorities.

These facts itself tell loudly that Batalik–Yaldor was Pakistan's most fortified area, but Indian Army gave them the deadliest reply with their bravery and courage.

1/11 GR, 12 JAKLI, Ladakh Scouts, 10 PARA SF, 17 GREN, 1 Bihar, and 22 GREN were deployed in sector.

Jubar Complex

On 29 May 1999, 1 Bihar was given the task to capture Jubar Complex. 1 Bihar was in Assam and coming straight to conflict zone in a totally different climate conditions than few days back (they inducted after war broke) in its previous field of posting. Same mistakes as we did in early days of Dras, mistakes were done here as well. The units were not logistically ready, as well as not properly acclimatised to high altitude. You can imagine a person's position that is coming straight into -10 to -30°C and high altitude conditions from Assam. But soldiers of Indian Army are not like ordinary men. They are committed to perform well in all odd, or whatsoever conditions are, so did Major Sarvanan.

On 20 May, Major M. Sarvanan assigned the task of capturing well-fortified Jubar top at almost 14,000 feet.

Major Sarvanan launched his assaults with his platoon. But very soon, they realised by actual ground position of enemy, which was very well established.

Sarvanan's bravery was unparalleled. He broke six levels of enemy resistance in his brave assault to the Jubar Top. In fact, even his own soldiers could not keep up with him. The youngster kept shooting, moving, and climbing. He almost captured the Jubar Top. He was unstoppable until the enemy fired a rocket, cutting him down. The hero of Batalik collapsed. Such was his bravery that for more than forty-five days later, repeated attempts by our troops failed to get the enemy post at peak and for a long time. Brave Major Sarvanan's body was still lying in battlefield. The most beautiful landscape of Batalik was becoming the most deadly.

The only survivor of this assault was Naik Shatrughan. Shatrughan was hit by three bullets in leg and somehow crawled back to base. He gave unit the information of how Major Sarvanan died after killing at least six to eight enemies and abandon their two bunkers in almost hand-to-hand combat.

The only son of his parents, Major Sarvanan was awarded by Vir Chakra for his supreme sacrifice and bravery.

The same type of mistakes resulted us same type of damages. The body of Major Sarvann was not recovered, same as Maj Adhikari's in Tololing. Heavy artillery fire and accurate gunfire from enemy, seating on top, resulted more casualties to us. Our artillery were not inducted full fledge. Enemy here was in such strength that Indian aircrafts and satellites on reconnaissance mission took pictures of helicopters flying. Pakistani Army established its administrating base near LOC at Muntho Dhalo and Sangruti to support the intrusion, and successfully helping them to sustain captured area.

Weather here was one more big issue. These heights of peak were at 14,000 to 16,000 with a freezing temperature and snow covered area.

When infantry soldiers began operations to recover a peak, a doctor, accompanied by a medical assistant and stretcher-bearers, moved just one step behind. The climb was tough and the progress slow. Troops, many of them from the plains of Uttar Pradesh and Bihar, needed to stop every ten steps to recover their breath. Even those belonging to the State of Jammu and Kashmir were not so acclimatised to the heights and ran out of breath.

Initially, the soldiers were ordered to push ahead despite being out of breath. But this led to cases of High Altitude Pulmonary Oedema (HAPO) and High Altitude Cerebral Oedema (HACO). Now, the doctor carried oxygen for soldiers running out of breath. And with most injuries—that of bullet and splinter wounds—the doctor or medical assistant even carry shell dressing, splints, painkillers, and morphine shots, so that first aid can be given on the spot itself, the doctor added. Officers said the doctors were a great morale booster. Once the soldiers knew that they would be taken care of immediately on being hit, they fought better. Casualties here had been many.[2]

Jubar is very picturesque and beautiful mountain, but was proven to be very deadly and difficult to Indian troops. Again, 1 Bihar was given the task to capture Jubar top and 17 GARHWAL was tasked to capture area Humps (one and two). The task of capturing Jubar top was matter of reputation. They already lost Major Sarvanan and other brave soldiers in assault with no victory sign yet.

The Jubar complex was still being held strongly by more 140 Pakistani soldiers.

The attacks on Jubar were preceded by concentrated artillery fire. In an innovative action, the division employed some 122 mm Grad multibarrel rocket launchers in a direct firing role to pulverise enemy defences. These launchers were deployed close to a pass on the Batalik–Kargil road where they were at the same height as the Jubar Complex. With great professional pride, the gunners saw their ammunition destroy the targets. Direct hits shattered several enemy sangars.

On 29 June, 1 Bihar launched its attack. Phase 1 of the attack went off as planned, and the Pakistanis were driven out from their sangars on the Jubar Observation Post (OP) on 30 June. A counter-attack by the enemy was repulsed after inflicting heavy casualties. Jubar Top, immediately north of Jubar OP, proved to be a tough nut to crack. Heavy exchanges of fire, continued between the contending troops throughout the next day, resulted in large numbers of casualties on both sides. A second attempt to capture Jubar Top on the night of 30 June with a fresh company was also unsuccessful.

Battle continued to next five days as well. Our army commanders tried each and every battle tactics by firing artillery and air strikes. Luckily, we hit the ammunition dump of enemy, and it made them weaker and thin. In a fresh attack, we captured Jubar Top in an attack led by Major K. P. R. Hari; and finally, Jubar falls. 1 Bihar also recovered large number of ammunition, enemy bodies, and other war documents. They also recovered bodies of Maj Sarvanan and three other soldiers.

It was a big pressure on Indian Army in early month of June to recapture Tololing and other adjoining peaks in Dras sector, but situation was now in under control over there and whole focus came to Batalik–Yaldor sector where situation was yet very bad and horrific.

Khalubar

On 30 June, 22 GREN launched attack on Point 5287 on Khalubar region. Maj Ajit Singh, commanding company with few expert mountaineer from Vikas Battalion, made a good attempt and succeeded in holding two good footholds on Khalubar region. Point 5287 was firmly held and secured now.

Later on 2 June 1999, 1/11 GR was deployed for the rest of task to capture Khalubar. Colonel Lalit Rai was commanding Rashtriya rifles deployed in counter-insurgency in Doda (J

& K). He got message from HQ to take control of 1/11 GR immediately, and Colonel Rai did it without thinking once. It was a great opportunity for him to command the unit, which his father commanded when he was colonel.

He immediately flew and reached Yaldor and took up the command in his hands. Gorkhas were always known for the obedience and bravery, but it was not easy for them to get familiar with their new CO. Colonel Rai needed to get confidence of soldiers and officers; thus, he decided to lead from front. He decided to lead the assault on Khalubar himself.

Now Gorkhas had to go for the final kill and capture Khalubar Top. They started climbing after heavy artillery fire from BOFORS, the mechanical hero of mountains.

The Rai and party were welcomed by enemy by extremely heavy machine gun fire from bunkers—at least ten bunkers with two machine guns each, as I mentioned earlier. Enemy was firing anti-aircraft bullets on them as Colonel Rai told in a lecture at Pune later.

Going forward was not only tough, but seemed impossible, and 1/11 GR were facing heavy casualties as well. But as we say, 'When going gets tough, tough gets going.'

Lt Manoj Panday observed the situation. He knew that keep hiding will be suicidal for them as time was running out, and it will be dawn soon. In daylight, they will be mere ducks sitting behind the boulders and rocks, and enemy will enjoy butchering them from top.

At time of advancing, Colonel Rai got hit by a splinter in knee and a bullet in thigh.

Here, Manoj Panday decided to destroy bunkers to protect and keep advancing the troops of 1/11 GR. He crawled near the bunker from where two machine guns were firing on them. At certain distance, he stood up and launched the grenades in the bunker and kept crawling to next bunker. He destroyed four bunkers, and silenced them by damaging them very badly with the grenades.

Undaunted and without caring for his grievous injuries, he continued to lead the assault on the fifth position, urging his men, and destroyed the same with a grenade. On his last attempt of destroying fifth bunker, the machine gun from another bunker pierced his body by 7.62 mm bullets.

His last words were 'Na chhodnu' ('don't spare them' in Gorkha language). Lt Manoj Panday gave his supreme sacrifice in the line of duty toward his motherland, India. His courage and bravery gave an advancing edge to the troops to capture Khalubar. Later, the president of India awarded PARAM VEER CHAKR to LT MANOJ PANDAY.

Seeing this courage and bravery of Lt Manoj Panday, the troops of 1/11 charged up; and after a deadly assault by almost running into enemy bunkers, Colonel Rai and his men captured the Khalubar Top.

Khalubar had been captured now, but problems were not over. The worst time was yet to come for Colonel Rai and few soldiers who left. Officer, JCO, and soldier of 1/11 were injured or died. Now bigger test was to keep hold on Khalubar Top, as enemy had made supply chain and routes to retreat the post. Pakistan charged back on Colonel Rai and his men, but got pushed by them very bravely, not once but twice.

Khalubar was very precious for Pakistan Army, and they made third attempt to recapture the top. This time, Colonel Rai was left with almost no ammunition, and there was no way to stop them. All of sudden, Colonel Rai made a contact back at base and ordered to open artillery fire upon top. It was a suicidal order, and thus refused by artillery office at first; but as it was order from CO who was fighting himself on front, they had no other option.

Colonel Rai and his men were spread, and hid themselves under boulders and rocks and bunkers made by enemy. Forwarding Pakistan troops were not expecting this idea of artillery fire at this time in their wildest dreams, and found themselves trapped till death. Colonel Rai's daring idea to open fire on top, which could have took their own lives, was a game changer. Colonel Rai showed example of great leadership, and he was awarded by VIR CHAKRA.

1/11 GR was bestowed with 'Bravest of Brave' title.

POINT 5203

On 6 July, 70 Infantry tasked 12 JAK LI along with a company of 5 PARA to recapture Point 5203. The assault was launched from Junk Lungpa Nala position. After an extensive artillery fire and heavy firing battalion secured a good position near Point 5203. Captain Kalia was the brave heart who assaulted the nearest enemy position (Point 5203) with mere handful men, and successfully managed to capture it. Next night, enemy counter-attacked in full throttle to capture this position, and this resulted in a hand-to-hand combat and were beaten back by our brave soldiers.

The enemy launched a second counter-attack, which was supported by artillery, machine guns, and RPGs from two directions at exactly 0300 hours on 9 June. It was a fierce fight, which followed in hand-to-hand fight. After his LMG crew was killed, Captain Kalia took over the LMG himself, shot down three enemy personnel, and injured three others. In spite of being badly wounded by burst of several bullets, Captain Kalia continued to fight till his death, but not before beating up the counter-attack and reinforcing of the position by our forces.

That day, we lost Captain Amol Kalia, Subedar Bahadur Singh, and Lance Naik Ghukam Mohammad Khan. All three were awarded Veer Chakra (Posthumous) for their act of great courage and bravery on that fateful night.

This was the battle that spanned for twelve days. Finally, on 20 June, company of 5 PARA and two companies of Karakoram Wing Ladakh Scouts launched a multidirectional attack on the feature, which made the enemy abandon its defenses and run for its lives. 0700 hour, 21 June 1999, point 5203 was recaptured.

POINT 4812

12 JAKLI was tasked to assault and capture 4812. Point 4812 is situated at southern extremity of Khalubar ridgeline. In this assault, Captain K. C. Nongrum and Havildar Satish Chander demonstrated outstanding gallantry while capturing the Point 4812. Captain Nongrum and seven other soldiers were killed. For next two days, unit held post; and by reinforcement, they captured the whole terrain. They also captured a Pakistani soldier alive, Naik Inayat Ali.

Kukarthang

1/11 GR launched attack at Kukarthang on 8 July. After heavy artillery and mortar fire, *A* company secured Point 4821 and *D* company secured Ring Contour, formation en route to Kukarthang Top. On early morning of 9 July, Kakarthang Top was all clear by our troops. Our troops recovered enemy dead bodies and their heavy storage of ammunition and ration.

Chorabat La

On 30 May 1999, a column of the Indus Wing, Ladakh Scouts, as a part of ongoing operations in the Batalik sector was tasked to occupy ridgeline on the line of control in a glaciated area at a height of about 5,500 metres. This was essential so as to preempt its occupation by the enemy and any subsequent infiltration.

The column of Indus wing was led by Major Sonam Wangchuk.

While moving toward the line of control, the enemy ambushed the column by firing from a vantage position. Major Sonam Wangchuk held his column together, and in a daring counter ambush, led a raid on the enemy position from a flank, killing two enemy soldiers. They also recovered one heavy machine gun and one universal machine gun, ammunition, controlled stores, and three dead bodies of the enemy personnel.

Two additional companies of Ladakh scouts were rushed to the area to occupy high features Point 5440, Point 5498, and Point 5520. By 2 June, Chorbat La ridgeline was totally secured. The Chief of Army Staff made a special instant award of 'Unit Citation' to Ladakh Scouts for their meritorious and gallant performance during the battle.

Major Sonam Wangchuk was awarded by MAHAVIR CHAKARA for displaying exceptional bravery and gallantry of the highest order in the presence of enemy fire and in extreme climatic conditions in the glaciated area.

14 Sikh was tasked to capture Point 5310 (17500 feet) on 22 July. The unit commando team led by Lieutenant Praveen Kumar accomplished this feat.

Turtuk Sector

Turtuk is located north of Chorbat La. Pakistan had plans to infiltrate militants into this area to subvert the locals and initiate insurgency. Timely action taken by Indian troops foiled their plan. In subsequent stages, Pakistan was to have launched operations to occupy critical areas around Turtuk, followed by heli-borne and airborne operations in rear areas; and finally, to integrate these areas with Pakistan's northern areas. Success would have cut off Siachen and the bases supporting it.

Subsector Haneef

At the end of May, 11 Rajputana Rifles, a battalion that was in the process of leaving after completing its tenure at the Central Glacier, was inducted through the Turtuk Lungpa to occupy defences on the LOC at point 5500 and adjacent areas. Here, personnel from 5 Vikas assisted 11 Rajputana Rifles. On 6-7 June, an attempt was made to capture point 5590 by a patrol led by Captain Haneef-ud-din, an Army Service Corps officer serving on attachment with 11 Rajputana Rifles. The patrol, moving at a height of 18,500 feet, approached the enemy position, but came under heavy fire. Despite grave injuries, Captain Haneef-ud-din took up position and kept on engaging the enemy till the remaining patrol succeeded in establishing a foothold on the mountain. He succumbed to his injuries thereafter. In recognition of this gallant young officer's determined leadership, the new sector occupied during Operation Vijay, south of Subsector West (SSW), was named Subsector Haneef (SSH). In this action, Naib Subedar Mangej Singh, who was assisting Haneef-ud-din on this patrol, conducted himself in an exemplary manner.

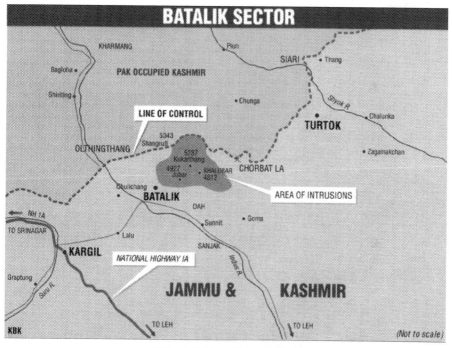

FIG: BATALIK SECTOR

Soldier Carrying Rocket Launcher Marching Towards
Given Assault Target With Its Coy

Point 4812 In The Kargil Region Which Persumably Saw
The Highest Casuality During Opreation Vijay.

The Victorious Indian Army Jawans of 18 Grenadiers rejoicing
with the National Flag in their hands after recapturing the Tiger
Hill in Drass sector of Jammu and Kashmir in 1999.

References

1. Kargil from Surprise to Victory by Gen V. P. Malik, Page no. 189
2. Dateline Kargil by Gaurav C. Sawant, Page no. 61
3. Kargil from Surprise to Victory by Gen V. P. Malik, Page no. 206
4. Page No. 60, Pakistan Strategic Blunder at Kargil by Gurmeet Kanwal

CHAPTER 10

MUSHKOH VALLEY

'Yeh Dil Mange More'
- Sher Shah

In Kargil war 'Sher shah' was code name given to Capt Vikram Batra, PVC 'Yeh Dil Mange More' was his company's coded massage for mission accomplish.

CHAPTER 10

Mushkoh Valley lies between LOC and Srinagar-Drass-Leh highway. The mountain features here are much higher than Dras. Mushkoh Valley saw highest number of infiltration activity other than any other sector laying on LOC. GULTARI, Pakistan's nearest army base, just thirty kilometres from LOC, was giving intruders more support and strength for their infiltration activities. Mushkoh Valley, as well, gave infiltrators a direct passage to DODA–KISHTWAR region of Jammu without entering Kashmir Valley.

Main area of intrusion in this region were Point 4875, Pimple 1 and 2, Twin Bumps, Whale Back.

Point 4875

Point 4875 was the enemy's most defended location in region. Point 4875 gave enemy a clear view of thirty kilometres along the NH-1A highway. It gave enemy an upper hand to restrict the movement on highway toward Dras and Leh. Forward observation post of enemy was giving a perfect coordination to their artilleries, and it was creating humongous domination in the region.

Pt 4875 dominates the national highway from Mugalpur to Dras, a stretch of approximately thirty kilometres. A feature called Rocky Knob links it with Tiger Hill. It provided an approach to the main administrative base of the enemy general area Point 4388, and formed a major hub of their defence. Its capture would seal the fact of the enemy operations in Mushkoh, and possibly act as catalyst in hastening their withdrawal. By 3 July, all preparations for the attack on Point 4875 were complete, and I met the Cdr and COs in the Bde HQ to do through the final plan. I was also satisfied to see the COs fully confident of accomplishing their task. By 3 July, last light, the two assault battalions (i.e., 17 JAT and 13 JAK RIF) had completed their recce and build-up and had moved into their forward assembly area, which for convenience was called Adm base, and which was somewhat midway to the objective.[1]

The task of recapturing of Point 4875 and other features were given to Mountain Brigade 79. 79 Mountain Brigade was led by Brg Ramesh Kakar.

These battalions were moved under 79 Mountain Brigade:

17 JAT, 13 JAK RIF—the heroes of Point 5140 in DRAS, 12 MAHAR, 2 NAGA, 21 SF

Point 4875 was divided into many parts, which were held by enemy. Commander decided to capture Whale Back, Pimple 1, Pimple 2, northern side (named Twin Bumps and Saddle), Southern Slope, and Flat Top in brigade level assault by a multidirectional attack.

2 NAGA, which had joined us earlier from valley, had done the recce of their objective area, as well as acclimatised themselves for their part of operation. Point 4875 was divided into many parts, which were held by the enemy, viz. Whale Back, Pimple 1, and Pimple 2; then there was Point 4875 Southern Slop and Flat Top; and the northern side was named Twin Bumps and Saddle.

The base of enemy defences was toward the east, south-east, and south-west. The plan of attack was thus planned from the south, which, in our perception, was the most unexpected approach. In Phase 1, 17 JAT was to capture Pimple 1 and Whale Back from the south by first light on 5 July, in the same phase 13 JAK RIF was to capture South Spur from south-east and Point 4875 from the south in the same time frame. A teamless squad of 2 SF was to establish a block along Safaid Nala; a company of MAHAR was to establish a firm base at Point 4540 and Tekri to interdict enemy between Twin Bumps and Point 4875. In phase 2, 17 JAT was to capture Pimple 2 by first light in 7 July, and exploit up to north spur; 13 JAKRIF was to capture Flat Top in the same time frame; and 2 NAGA was to capture Twin Bumps by first light in 7 July and exploit toward north-west.[2]

On the D-day, July-4, Colonel G. S. Maan, the commanding officer of 105 mm field gun unit, was supervising the preparation of artillery attack on Point 4875.

As soon as sun drooped in west, artillery started its job of pounding TNT shells and splinters on feature for next several hours.

Meanwhile, companies of 13 JAK RIF and 17 JAT started climbing (and NAGA also).

13 JAK RIF started assault with one company led by Major S. Vijay Bhasker, and another company led by Major Gurpreet Singh. Captain Vikram Batra was assigned to give cover fire by MMG from firebase.

By attacking from two sides, 13 JAK RIF marched to surprise and divide the attention of enemy. Gradually, they were coming close to the objective.

On other hand, 17 JAT was also headed toward its task to capture Pimple 1 and Whale Back. Company was led by Major Ritesh Sharma. Young dynamic, Lt Anuj Nayyar, was also in company led by Major Ritesh. All of sudden, Major Ritesh got injured in enemy shelling. Now, responsibility of leading the company was on Anuj's shoulders.

Nayyar told his troops to wait till he silenced the machine gun. The soldiers volunteered to accompany him, but he refused. 'More men mean more chance to being seen. Wait here,' he ordered. Through twice his age, the soldier obeyed the officer and waited behind a rock. Nayyar crawled on all fours. The machine gun was aimed at his face, but he did not get scared. He continued to crawl till he was under the machine gun nest. Still crouching, he pulled out a grenade and lobbed it inside the hole where the gun was kept and ran back. With a loud bang, the grenade went off, silencing the machine gun. Gradually climbing and crossed Pimple 1 feature successfully. His men, awed by their young commander's bravery, followed.[3]

Still, task was not fully finished. Irony of combined attack was that if one fails, other partly suffers; and this was very clear in mind of Captain Anuj that if he fails, then 13 JAK RIF and 2 NAGA would be in trouble. He decided to capture Whale Back as soon as possible, and encouraged his troops to move forward. Enemy had a heavy machine gun post here. They caught enemy by surprise, and dislodged them from post by capturing it.

13 JAK RIF was also moving forward, and by the dawn, they were at the top of Point 4875. Colonel Joshi was still very tense because biggest problem in high altitude was to reinforce troops. Obviously, troops on top were restless, wounded, and short of ammunition. To making the scenario worst, few of features were still in hand of enemy. From there, they could counter-attack easily. Any movement in day for our troop was no less than a suicide. Pakistan artillery, too, opened in daylight to make situation much darker for us.

Indian victory would not have been complete without the capturing of feature Flat Top. A young rifleman, Sanjay Kumar of 13 JAK RIF, volunteered himself to capture Flat Top.

Rifleman Sanjay Kumar

Rifleman Sanjay Kumar volunteered to be the leading scout of the attacking column tasked to capture area Flat Top of Point 4875 in the Mushkoh Valley on 4 July 1999. Enemy automatically fire from one of the sangars posed stiff opposition and stalled the progress of the column. Rifleman Sanjay Kumar charged the enemy sangar with utter disregard for his personal safety. In the ensuing hand-to-hand combat, he killed three Pakistani soldiers and was, himself, seriously injured. However, despite his injuries, he continued to fight and charged attack. The enemy fled from the scene, leaving behind one machine gun. Although Rifleman Sanjay Kumar was bleeding profusely from his wounds, he refused to be evacuated. His actions motivated his comrades to capture area Flat Top from the enemy. For his most conspicuous gallantry against heavy odds leading to the capture of an important objective, Rifleman Sanjay Kumar was awarded the Param Vir Chakra, India's highest gallantry award.[4]

But Pakistan wanted to turn each and every stone to recapture Flat Top. Young Captain N. A. Nagappa was holding Flat Top. First counter-attack of Pakistan was beaten back. Indian troops were reposing very heavily on enemy troops waiting to climb forward to Flat Top captured by us.

All of a sudden, a splinter pierced through both legs of Captain Nagappa. This gave an advantage to enemy to move forward faster. Enemy's supply chain needs to be cut very badly, or else the sacrifice of so many lives will go in vain.

Sher Shah (the code name of Captain Vikaram Batra) was silently observing the situation from base, and suddenly went to his CO and volunteered himself to capture the enemy post, which was continuously firing on trapped Indian troops.

The Bravery of Captain Vikram Batra

On 7 July 1999, Vikram 'Sher Shah' started the assault with loading his men from front. He was not fit and recovering from his injuries he got in capturing 5140. It was dark night and heavy fog was giving a good cover to our advancing troops. Sher Shah and his men were advancing by crawling on their all four when all of sudden, a burst of fire came upon like a rain shower on them. Enemy spotted them. Now, there was no other alternate than starting fire on enemy bunker. They needed to be silenced somehow; or if this engaged them till morning, the enemy will easily spot them and then it will be a knife in butter for them to spot our troops and kill them by sitting on top.

Batra charged up himself to first bunker in rain of bullets fired by enemy machine gun, and lobbed grenades in bunker and silenced them by killing all four enemy soldier. Now, his next target was second bunker of narrow ridge on mountain.

The trapped Indian soldier grabbed the chance of charging on enemy. Batra and his men charged on second bunker with the battle cry of JAK RIF, 'DURGA MATA KI JAI'. Batra lunged inside the bunker and killed the entire enemy by point blank. Batra was literally signing the death warrants of enemy and executing them instantly. By the ferocity of assault, enemy was so much scared that they started running toward their territory, leaving behind their guns and injured soldier, but Batra was not in mood to let them flee. He, with his men, were chasing the enemy like a tiger and picking them with his gun.

'There was a time he grappled with a Pakistani soldier, punching him in the nose. As soon as he fell, Batra plunged his bayonet into the fallen soldier's stomach. But another enemy soldier caught him from behind. He, too, was done to death after being thrown off the back by Batra, the ferocious. All hell broke loose. It was utter chaos,' a soldier of JAKRIF, who accompanied him in the attack, said. Seven Pakistanis were killed in the attack.[5]

He turned around to boost the morale of his men when the fleeing enemy fired on him. He was badly injured. Vikram Batra succumbed to his injuries. For his unparalleled feats of gallantry, leadership, and selfless devotion, Captain Vikram Batra was awarded the India's highest gallantry award, 'PARM VIR CHAKRA'.

At this time, Captain Sashi Bhushan Ghildiyal, the forward observation officer, took over company. He and Havildar Kumar Singh fought bravely. One company was sent by base to reinforce them.

Throughout the acting, Colonel Umesh Singh Bawa set an example of leadership in beating back the enemies' counter-attacks on Pimple 2.

2 NAGA were assigned to capture Twin Bumps. Their assault was planned in next phase; they got more time to prepare, as well as less resistance of enemy. On 6 July, Twin Bumps were recaptured.

The enemy had now been effectively evicted from all his positions close to highway in the Mushkoh Valley sector.

Kaksar Sector

Most of the area of this region is glaciated. The mountains here are more than 15,000 feet. The main ridge is compromising Point 5608, Point 5605, and Point 5280.

The only intrusion in area was capturing of Bajrang post by enemy (Point 5299).

On 14 May 1999, a five-men patrol was sent to check the intrusion in area. Patrol went disappeared and was reported missing.

After almost one month, Pakistan Army returned the bodies of our soldiers. The conditions of bodies were very bad, and there were clear signs of being tortured and mutilation before shooting them from very close range.

When the media reported this incident in newspapers and other information portals, whole nation got upset and full of anger.

After patrol led by Sourabh Kalia reported missing, 4 Jat sent another patrol led by Amit Bhardwaj.

They also got trapped by enemy and were fired upon. One soldier was killed and ten were wounded in this incident. Body of Amit Bhardwaj and another soldier was recovered after one month.

On 17 May, another patrol was launched by 4 Jat led by Maj Vikram Shekhawat. They gained a major foothold on point 5299. Major Vikram was wounded in this assault.

After these incidents, Indian Army planned a brigade level attack to recapture Bajrang Post (Point 5299).

This full-fledged operation was resumed because of ceasefire announced, and Pakistan Army offered withdrawal. On 15 July, our troops occupied positions in this area.

End of Military Operations

When military operations in Kargil ended on 26 July 1999, the Indian Army had captured eight Pakistani army soldiers and a large number of weapons, ammunition, equipment, and documents. Some details are now given.

Weapons and Ammunition Captured in War

Sr	Name	Qty
1	12.7 mm anti-aircraft machine guns	4
2	Universal/medium/general purpose machine guns	40
3	Heavy machine guns with tripods	9
4	Rifles (G3/AK/Chinese/M16/auto/SLR)	80
5	Rocket launchers (RPG)	14
6	Automatic grenade launchers	5
7	Mortars (81 mm/51 mm/60 mm)	10
8	120 mm mortars	3
9	Sniper rifles	6
10	23 mm gun	1
11	14.5 mm KPVT	1
12	PIKA machine gun	4
13	37 mm twin barrel air defence (AD) gun	1
14	Stinger missile with launcher	2
15	105 mm howitzers	3
16	Assorted ammunition	6 Tons
17	Mines	4432
18	Grenades	952

Prisoners of War

Sr	Name	Unit
1	Naik Inayat Ali	5 Northern Light Infantry
2	Sepoy Huner Shah	-do-
3	Sepoy Sher Baz Khan	-do-
4	Sepoy Mohammad Ayaz	-do-
5	Sepoy Fazal Aman	24 Sind
6	Sepoy Abdul Hamid	33 Frontier Force (FF)
7	Sepoy Salik Khan	-do-
8	Sepoy Ashraf	19 Frontier Force (FF)

(Source: Kargil From Surprise To Victory By Gen. V. P. Malik page no. 211 & 216)

The following Indian Army units, which performed admirably, were awarded the COAS' Unit Citation (an appreciation from chief of army staff) in the Kargil War:

- 8 Sikh
- 13 JAK Rifles
- 1 Bihar
- 17 Jat
- Ladakh Scouts
- 18 Garhwal Rifles
- 1/11 Gorkha Rifles
- 2 Naga
- 18 Grenadiers
- 12 JAK Light Infantry
- 663 Recce and Observation Squadron
- 141 Field Regiment
- 2 Rajputana Rifles
- 666 Recce and Observation Squadron
- 108 Medium Regiment
- 197 Field Regiment

References

1. KARGIL TURNING THE TIDE, Lt Gen Mohinder Puri Page no. 95
2. KARGIL TURNING THE TIDE, Lt Gen Mohinder Puri, Page no. 96
3. Dateline Kargil, Gourav Sawant, Page no. 182
4. Kargil from Surprise to Victory, Gen V. P. Malik, Page no. 179
5. Dateline Kargil, Gourav Sawant, Page no. 187

CHAPTER 11

OPERATION SAFED SAGAR

'Nabhah Sprsam Diptam'*

(Touch the Sky with Glory)

---

*   *Nabhah Sprsam Diptam (नभः स्पृशं दीप्तम्) is motto of Indian Air Force

CHAPTER 11

'The fifth floor of the headquarters of the Indian Air Force (IAF) is the power centre of the air force. On a hot summer morning in 1999, I, a wing commander then, was busy with my nose dug deep in some file when the buzzer sounded twice in quick succession. That was unusual. As a staff officer to the Chief of the Air Staff (CAS) and whose job was to manage his secretariat, two quick buzzes meant the boss was in a hurry. I yanked the phone from its cradle and said, "Sir?" Air Chief Marshal Anil Yashwant Tipnis said, "Get JD (H) and you to come along with him." On the intercom, I asked Group Captain Anthony, the joint director of the helicopter fleet, to come quickly to the chief's office. He queried, "What's up?" as the Chief normally doesn't call a joint director for consultation. I said that I didn't know, but the Vice Chief of Army Staff (VCOAS) had asked for an urgent meeting, and was inside the office with him. It was around ten in the morning on Friday, 14 May 1999. While the IAF knew that something was not right up North, it was about to learn that things were really amiss in the desolate heights over Kargil,' Air Vice Marshal Manmohan Bahadur writes in his article.

In recent past, no war has been won without control of the airs pace in which operations are conducted. Indian Army also requested for air support in Kargil War. Indian Air Force and Indian Army showed a great example of coordination, and it helped a lot in turning the tide of Kargil War.

Air Chief Marshal Anil Tipnis was commanding air force at the time of Kargil War. He, himself, flew fighter planes in conflict zone. The air force operation in Kargil War was given code name 'OPERATION SAFED SAGAR'.

It was a huge task for IAF to give support required for Indian Infantry units in battle region.

The terrain in and around Kargil is between 4,572 metres and 5,486 metres above sea level. The aircraft are, therefore, required to fly at altitudes of about 6,100 metres. The density of the air at these heights is roughly 30 per cent less than that of the air at sea level. This causes a reduction in the weight that can be carried, and also the pilot's ability to manoeuvre as the radius of a turn is higher here than at lower levels. Also, engine performance deteriorates with altitude; as for the same forward speed, a smaller mass of air goes into the jet engine of the fighter or the engine of the helicopter compared to low altitudes. The non-standard air density also affects the trajectory of weapon.[1]

In early day of May, this was the time when army was totally confused and having no idea about area of intrusions who are the intruders and what was there strength at peaks. Army asked for help from air force. Indian Army wanted the actual position of intruders on the peaks, and if any support they were getting from beyond the position they were holding.

On 21 May, air force sent their first Canberra aircraft on reconnaissance mission in Batalik sector. Sq leader, U. K. Jha, was navigating the plane, and Sqn leader A. Perumal was flying the plane. Ninety minutes pass, they reached over Batalik from Agra Airbase from where they started. As soon as they reached over peaks, Sq leader U. K. Jha started taking pictures. The very first expression on his face was horrific. The peaks were under heavy intrusion, and few bases were also established under our side of line of control by enemy. Sqn leader U. K. Jha request Sqn leader Perumal to fly over Batalik regions once again, so that he can get one more chance to capture the enemy activity in our area. As they were flying over Batalik region, all of sudden they felt shattered by knowing that they were hit by enemy's anti-aircraft missile.

Sqn leader Perumal calmed himself, and somehow managed the control of aircraft. He landed safely at Srinagar Airbase. The pictures taken by them were more than enough for army HQ to feel an earthquake of 10.0 magnitude. They were clearly showing the bunker/*sangers* and intruders in a large numbers.

After the meeting on 24 May of CCS at New Delhi, the Cabinet Committee on Security authorized the IAF to mount attacks on the infiltrators without crossing the LOC. As per plan, air force will send its fighter planes, as well as bombing the identified location on hills and supply bases of intruders, and then photo reconnaissance mission capture the real situation and damage done by IAF on peaks captured.

On 26 May, Golden Arrow (17 Squadron of Indian Air Force based at Bhatinda, Punjab, known as Golden Arrow) Wg. Cdr. B. S. Dhanoa (Tony) and R. S. Dhaliwal also took off in the morning for a recce of Tiger Hill and Tololing. The film revealed snow tents with artillery hits around them. Strikes also began on this day

Flying from the Indian air fields of Srinagar, Avantipur and Udhampur ground attack aircraft MiG-21s, MiG-23s, MiG-27s, Jaguars, and the Mirage 2000 were ready now struck insurgent positions. The very first time, fighter aircrafts were given order to fire on enemy after the 1971 war.

The Initial Setback

Initially, Indian Air Force got major setbacks by loosing MIG-17, MIG-27, and MI17 in operations. These incidents are as follows:

Ajay Ahuja and Nachiketa (MIG-17 and MIG-27 incident)

Flt Lt Nachiketa was number four in air attack mission with his MIG-27, followed by Squadron leader Ajay Ahuja with his MIG-21. Ajay Ahujas task was to take pictures of damage done by our air strike. Flt Lt Nachiketa, or Nachi as he was known, while flying, hit the target perfectly. But he was not confident about the accuracy, so instead of coming back to base, he made loop over target and bombed it again; and at this crucial moment, his aircraft's engine reported a flame out. In a hustle bustle, Nachi tried to control the aircraft, but lost the altitude and throw himself out of aircraft by ejecting system. Fnt Lt Nachiketa landed safely, but got caught by enemy. Sqn Ldr Ajay Ahuja saw Nachiketa ejected and flew very low on the location of incident happen. He was very much concerned about his safety, but flying low made him an easy target of enemy missile. Sqn Ldr Ajay's aircraft got damaged, and Ajay ejected himself and was shot dead by enemy soldiers when he was landing with his parachute nearby an enemy post.

Air Attack on Tololing

Air force planned its first air strike on 28 May in Batalik sector. There were so many problems air force was facing in Kargil battle to make offence on peaks. It was not easy to target the peaks by fighter jet, and then thin air. Higher altitude was another problem, which causes lack of accuracy. Weather and terrain was also problematic in finding the targets, so air force decided to indulge war helicopters.

MI-35 in battle, India Air Force had only MI-35 as war helicopter. This could carry missiles and rockets. Problem was not over. MI-35 could fly up to 10,000 only and target (intrusion area on peaks) was at around 15,000. No other option was left, so AF decided to make shift some changes in MI-17 to get its work done.

MI-17 helicopter was used for transportation of logistic and troops only. It has a capacity of flying at max 18,000 height—more than sufficient for air strike in region. 4UB32 rocket pods with 55–57 mm rockets were attached and tested. Results were positive.

MI-17 of 129 Nubra Warriors and 152 HU were given the task of air strike at Batalik region under command of Wing Commander A. K. Sinha.

Nubra 1, 2, 3, 4 were ready to strike at Point 5140. Under given preparation, they found that infrared flaming function with some helicopter from any heat seeking strike was not working.

Sinha advised Flt Lt S. Muhilan to stay on ground, but Muhilan refused with respect and requested to fly. Flt Lt Rajiv Pundir volunteered himself to fly with Muhilan as co-pilot.

In a perfect coordination, they were flying and started the air strike on Point 5140, damaging targets very badly. But similar type of mistake was done by air force as initially done by Indian Army, underestimating the enemy. Enemy shot the S. Muhilan's MI-17 by stringer missile. ANZA MK II, which is guided by infrared heat seeker. S. MUHILAN and Sqr Ldr Rajiv Pundir, with Sergeant PVNR Prasad and Sergeant Raj Kishor Sahu, died. Later, all four were awarded by Vayu Sena Medal (POSTHUMOUS).

As I have mentioned in earlier chapter, IAF was in shock because of early setbacks, loss of MIG-21 and MI-27 of Flt Lt Nachilketa and Sqn Ldr Ajay Ahuja. MI-17 incident added more tensions to Air Force HQ. At this point, it was confirmed that intruders were regular army persons and not terrorist. They had all the ammunition and guns to counter-attack any air strike of Indian Air Force.

Soon, it was realised that operation in this region required special tactics because of terrain. Attacks on small mountains are not easy; sometimes even very hard to see them with naked eyes. Even when a target had been spotted, it was difficult to hit it accurately with 500 and 1,000 pound free flight bombs and rockets. Shoulder-fired missiles were also a big threat as well. It was decided to not use any low flying machine near or above peaks, which can be easily targeted by enemy seating on peaks. Air strikes were on hold for few days, and it was decided to launch operation after a better assessment of enemy location and weapon.

Revenge of the pilots who lost their lives in early days of war was still due. Air force decided to strike on enemy by Kings of Air force, Mirage and Jaguar, the best fighter planes of Indian Air Force.

By the mid of June, picture was getting clear. Most of the intrusions were detected and areas were identified. The army was now in a position to make an air strike plan on the particular targets before assaults, the air force was more able to coordinate with the army for the 'close air support' requirements.

As of 12 July 1999, Indian Air Force fighters had flown approximately 580 strike missions, supported by around 460 air defence missions like Combat Air Patrol and escorts, and about 160 reconnaissance sorties, amounting to a total of approximately 1,200 sorties.

Air Strikes by MIRAGE

After repeated bomb and rocket runs by IAF MIG-21s and MiG-27s had failed to dislodge heavily entrenched Pakistani defences well within Indian Territory. The IAF played its trump card—the surgical strikes by Mirages were started by first week of June. Laser-guided bombs, a new makeshift innovation for MIRAGE by IAF, broke the back of the enemy's supply lines. In fact, only at MUNTHO DHALO, a Pakistan Army supply base, suffered more than 180 casualties in deadly strikes of Indian Air Force.

Significant air strikes that altered the course of the conflict:

1. 13 June 1999, Tololing Ridge Complex in the Batalik Sector
2. 17 June 1999, Muntho Dalo, the main admin and Logistic camp in the Batalik sector
3. 24 June 1999, command and control structure on Tiger Hill, direction centre for forward artillery in the Dras Sector
4. 23 June 1999, logistics camp at Point 4388 in Mushkoh Nallah

Other than air strikes, IAF played major role in taking airlift in the form of casualties, evacuation, and fresh reinforcement in which MI-17 played a major role. For the first time, an Indian woman helicopter pilot flew in war zone.

For the first time, on 4 July, a strike was made on a supply camp, and gun positions situated at Point 4388 of the Drass sector. These attacks resulted successful destruction of gun position, and the the enemy supply chain, too, was shattered. The attacks proved that with a good recon air strikes, indeed, were an example of lethal strikes. Further attacks were continued with Mirages on the sixth and tenth of July. These attacks broke the enemy backbone with a high casualty rate. The success of these attacks could be concluded by the fact that by 9 July, our army recaptured almost all (99 per cent exactly) of Batalik sector, whereas only 10 per cent of the Drass sector (capturing 90 per cent of it) was left to be conquered.

Chief of Army staff General VP Malik and Air Chief Marshal AY Tipnis with Indian Army soldiers in Kargil sector that they visited.

References

1. The Hindu Saturday, 19 June 1999 Narendra Gupta, former Air Vice-Marshal

CHAPTER 12

OPERATION TALWAR

'Sham No Varunah'*

(May the Lord of the water be auspicious unto us.)

---

*   Sham No Varunah (शं नो वरुणः) is motto of Indian Navy.

CHAPTER 12

'Operation Talwar' was the code name given to operation of Indian Navy during the Kargil War.

Navy's contributions were less visible during the war, but operation Talwar was an important factor that helped us in winning war.

Admiral Sushil Kumar was commanding the Indian Navy during the war.

After CCS meeting on 24 May, operation Talwar was launched. The Western Naval Command deployed INS TARAGIRI on patrolling near Dwarka, the city that was badly hit by Pakistan in 1965 war. But this time, navy decided to not take any chance, and was not in mood of giving an opportunity to Pakistan. A major combat force was deployed at Saurashtra (Gujarat) for creating some pressure, and giving enemy a clear offensive message by adopting an openly hawkish posture.

Admiral Sushil Kumar ordered Western Naval Command to increase patrolling, and missile ships were ordered to sail just outside the Pakistan waters.

This was first time that Pakistan realised that the Indian Navy warships were lurking outside the Karachi Coast. Memories of Karachi blockade and the burning city in December 1971 came alive. Pakistani aircraft saw the warships. 'And soon, a signal went out to all Pakistan navy ships to stay clear of the Indian navy vessels. The loop we wanted to make outside Karachi was more or less complete,' Rear Admiral Bangara said in a conversation with journalist and writer, Gaurav Sawant. From 1 to 11 June, the situation in Kargil was tense. More and more troops and weapons were being deployed, but the army continued to suffer losses. With the IAF sorties lessened after the initial loss, the Pakistan Air Force (PAF) was on red alert.[1]

Our navy's dominant role and hawkish posture pushed Pakistan on back foot. The arm-twisting of Pakistan by our navy was not over. On 15 June, more ships were deployed just few nautical miles away off the coast of Karachi.

Although the Western Naval Command is more than sufficient to deal with Pakistan Force and capability, ratio is 1:7 in favour of Indian Navy, but still, to create more pressure on Pakistan Eastern Fleet was ordered to move.

Pakistan's economy survives on its oil and trade from gulf region, which flows through its maritime lane. Pakistan has limited coastline. At the time of Kargil War, it has only two ports—Karachi and Quasim. Its civil and army's need of oil and petroleum was dependent on this coastline. Pakistan has only three major oil refineries; the major ones are Karachi and Rawalpindi. Pakistan does not have large state owned tankers like India; therefore, its sea transit and transportation was dependent on foreign vassals, which need to be requestioned by Pakistan. Any movement of Pakistan Navy through these ports were already under threat because of Indian Navy's aggressive deployment.

Pakistan strategic oil reserves are limited to some days. Indian reserves, whereas have the capacity to handle civil and military need based demands. Pakistan's 80 percent oil reserve flow through gulf; thus, proving it to be a vital lifeline for its economic needs, which were under arrest because Indian Navy's warship deployment in region. This made situation more vulnerable for Pakistan.

References

1. **Dateline Kargil, by gorav sawant, page no. 270**
2. **The Silent Sentinel, Maj Gen Ashok Mehta**

CHAPTER 13

ROLE OF ARTILLERY

Sarvatra Izzat-o-Iqbal
(Everywhere with Honour and Glory)

Sarvatra Izzat-o-Iqbal is motto of India Artillery

CHAPTER 13

Role of Artillery

IN MOUNTAIN WARFARE, THE INFANTRY SPEARHEADS THE ATTACKS, BUT THE SPEARHEADS HAS TO HAVE A STRONG SHAFT. THAT IS NONE OTHER THAN THE ARTILLERY - Gen V. P. Malik

In Operation Vijay, artillery firepower plays a major part in achieving victory in the battlefield. Success of our artillery is written in golden letters in Operation Vijay. It was a major threat for enemy, and it caused a major destruction to enemy's posts.

Accurate artillery fire degrades the enemy's defence, and continues heavy artillery firebreak their will to fight. Artillery fire on enemy's supply and reinforcement reduced enemy's fighting potential before a physical assault is launched. The artillery helped to reduce the casualties suffered by assaulting infantrymen.

Innovative idea of induction 155 mm FH 77-B Bofors, 105 mm field guns, 160 mm and 120 mm Mortars, and 122 mm GRAD BM-21 multibarrel rocket launchers into forward guns positions for direct fire on enemy was turning point of Operation Vijay.

The enhanced reach and versatility of weapons and ammunition now available could give the artillery enough opportunity to cause destruction and damage in a more effective and responsive manner than had been possible in the past. Nearly fifty fire units compromising artillery guns, howitzers, mortars, and one rocket battery were employed in the area of operations for various purposes: for destroying given objectives, for supporting the infantry attacks (described earlier), and for carrying out counter-bombardment. In all, these units fired nearly 250,000 rounds/rockets over a period of ninety days. The medium guns fired nearly 30 per cent of the total ammunition. Sometimes, in a space of five minutes, over 1,200 rounds of high explosives were fired on objectives such as Point 4875, Tololing, and Tiger Hill.[1]

Kargil has often been called a classic gunner's war. Artillery played a very important role in Kargil War. Operation Vijay was an example of high intensity operation in high altitude. It was supported by large amount of artillery fire.

There were so many incidents when company commanders became the victims of casualty. The FOO (Forward Observation Officer) took command of an assault, and get done the given task of capturing a part or peak.

Three hundred guns, MBRL, and motars were deployed, which fired approximately 5,000 shells including artillery shells, rockets, and bombs daily. The day Tiger Hill was recaptured, the quantum of 9,000 shells were fired on it. For sixteen to seventeen days continuously, during peak assault periods, the rate of fire was one shell per minute. Since World War II, such high rate of artillery fire was never witnessed.

The men worked relentlessly with sleepless night. Few of them only got two hours to rest in twenty-four hours. They even suffered blisters in their hand while carrying artillery shells. They even could not have proper meals. They also were under enemy counter artillery bombardment and fire. No better soldiers can any army produce as these men who showed selflessness and courage in face of enemy. The fact is proved that artillery was the prime killer since maximum casualty was rendered by artillery fire; hence, it is called the God of War.

The gunners equaled the infantry comrades in terms of courage, professionalism, and determination. Never in the previous wars were such challenges ever faced by the Indian Artillery. Young FOO and battery commanders fired accurately and gave sustained fire, while fighting shoulder to shoulder alongside infantry. The accuracy of artillery is well defined by the fact of safety distance which was forty meter given to infantry. This not only helped the infantry soldiers on ground, but also pinned down enemy heads before our infantry closed in to the enemy bunkers on mountain top.

These immaculate actions were under the able command of Brig Lakhwinder Singh who was commanding 8 Mountain Artillery Brigade.

Bofors In Action.

Artillery in Action

References

1. Kargil From Surprise To Victory, By Gen V. P. Malik, Page No. 221
2. Artillery, the Battle-Winning Arm, By Maj Gen Jagjit Singh, Page No. 116
3. Artillery, the Battle-Winning Arm, By Maj Gen Jagjit Singh, Page No. 11

CHAPTER 14

DIPLOMATIC WAR

'We will continue to operate with maximum restraint. We are a responsible member of the international community, and we shall continue to be so.'

- Jaswant Singh (At the Time of Kargil War)

CHAPTER 14

India won the Kargil war on both military and diplomatic front. Nations worldwide and media openly exposed Pakistan's provocation and its military's intrusions in Indian Territory.

US has taken a lead in labelling Pakistan as the aggressor nation. US media wrote about Pakistan's direct army role in Kargil intrusion.

Pakistan has lost more from Kargil than India has won. Pakistan was beaten badly on ground of battle and diplomatic front as well.

How India proved its view in front of world forum, and how we managed to get support of world leaders and their countryman? The answers lies within External Affairs Ministry of India under leadership of its external affairs minister, Mr Jaswant Singh*. MEA's strong advocacy on our point of Pakistan's aggression, and intrusion in our territory in front of world, made them think about Pakistan's bad intensions against peace and humanity.

In first week of May, when intrusions were detected, Jaswant Singh called his MEA officers and briefed them about the issue and given specific tasks. Their main task was to put across to the international community in as clear terms as possible that Kargil was aggression on India.

Jaswant Singh's clear line of thinking enthused the team. 'It is a fact that the Pakistani diplomats succeeded in convincing the world about their point of view in the past. They acted more confident, and at the same time, giving the impression of being hurt by big brother, India, bullying the little kid, Pakistan. The world sympathy was naturally with the underdog, and by the

---

* **Jaswant Singh is an Indian politician. He earlier belonged to the Bharatiya Janata Party and has held many portfolios in the national cabinet including Finance, External Affairs and Defence during the NDA regime. He also served India Army as an officer (Major) in his young age'**

time the bumbling Indian diplomats woke up and mumbled their side, the world decision-makers were already hostile,' MEA sources confided talking about Pakistan's abetment of cross-border tourism.[1]

On other hand, he started attending war room meetings with army leadership. As a fauji, his knowledge about an army operation and confidence, which army leadership need, helped government of India to understand the strategy of army operation and gave them the support needed accordingly. He used to remark that the south block has become one entity. It is like one body with two arms, MOD and MEA.

MEA made very clear that only solution of the situation was to respect the LOC, and Pakistan should back off from Indian Territory immediately.

It was Jaswant Singh who was able to get key countries to see India's viewpoint through some swift diplomatic moves.

He went to China and Russia on diplomatic tours. US deputy secretary of state, Strobe Talbot also met him. Talbot was aware of ongoing situation, but Jaswant Singh firmly put India's point that Pakistan was misleading the world with its lies. Talbot was sympathetic, but Singh made it very clear that India wanted US to do more than just click of tongue.[2]

In mid-June 1999, when fighting on the Tololing feature was still going on, Brajesh Mishra told his US counterpart, Sandy Berger, that India could no longer keep its armed forces on leash, and that an escalation of the conflict could not be ruled out. Prime Minister Vajpayee, too, threatened to carry the fighting beyond the LOC if Pakistan did not withdraw its forces from Jammu and Kashmir.

Meanwhile, the Ministry of External Affairs released a detailed statement on the situation. The ministry also conducted press briefing on Kargil. India's permanent representative to the UN conducted several briefing. Our embassies were also engaged, particularly in Washington, and our ambassador there undertook briefings to US media.

Jaswant Singh writes in his book, *In Service of Emergent India,* 'Madeline Albright then called me on May 30 to express her regret about developments in Kargil, and to indicate that she had spoken to Nawaz Sharif. She told me that the United States knew full well how the chain of events had started. She did hint at the possibility of a ceasefire, following which a withdrawal of troops would be possible. India had gone down that road several times earlier, and had learned that a ceasefire under such conditions was always converted into a ploy for remaining in occupation of the land being encroached upon, leading to endless, fruitless, and largely purposeless dialogue. I offered to Albright that were the Pakistan Government to restore the *status quo ante*, then we certainly would examine the feasibility of a ceasefire. She expressed some apprehension that things could get out of control. It was important, she said, to initiate a dialogue. In response, I said that we never averse to a dialogue, and never would be in future either, but we found it difficult to agree to such a step, so long as an aggression was still being committed against India and the aggressor was still on Indian land.[3]

By the first week of June, it was very clear to every country and UN that India will not initiate ceasefire or any negotiation until Pakistan withdraw its army from our land, and have rights to accelerate its effort to throwing them out. This clear stand forced UN, US, and other countries to take a stand. In result, each and every considerable country were supporting India and viewed that the restoration of confidence between the two countries will not be possible without putting an end to the violation of LOC, and to the intrusion of the past weeks in Indian Territory, as per Shimla Agreement.

China, 1 July, public call for India and Pakistan to earnestly respect the line of control in Kashmir was a particular heavy blow to Pakistan's increasingly isolated government.[5]

On 5 June, Russia joined in the fray. Predictably siding with India, Moscow asked Pakistan to restore the status quo on the LOC that existed before Pakistan's military intrusion, and stated that the Kashmir issue should be resolved through political dialogue between New Delhi and Islamabad. Russia also tried to apply pressure on Pakistan by issuing a stern warning through its embassy in Islamabad and official envoys that Pakistan's forces must immediately withdraw.[6]

On other hand, Pakistan was still trying its best to convince the world that it were Mujahidins actually who were capturing the peaks, not their regular army, and that it is not a conflict between India and Pakistan. World leaders and UN should intervene in real problem, which is Kashmir. They also tried to play a bilateral talk card and sent their Foreign Minister Sartaj Aziz to India for any chance of peace negotiations and ceasefire. On diplomatic front, it was very obvious to accept this request of foreign minister Level meeting in this war type situation. But Nawaz never thought, in his wildest dreams, what his foreign minister was going to face in India. Venue of meeting was decided New Delhi on 12 June.

Jaswant Singh was ready with, which I call a coffin for Pakistan Army's so-called good face.

On 11 June, Jaswant Singh called a press conference at his office and released a statement to press.

STATEMENT AT PRESS BRIEFING IN DELHI, 11 JUNE 1999

Foreign Minister Sartaj Aziz will be visiting Delhi tomorrow. His visit is taking place in the context of Pakistan's armed intrusion and aggression in the Kargil sector of Ladakh in Jammu and Kashmir.

I wish to share with you, ladies and gentlemen of the media, and through you with all the citizens of our country, as also the international community, some—and I repeat that this is only some—of the incontrovertible evidence that we have obtained about many aspects of this armed intrusion and aggression in the Kargil sector. This establishes beyond any doubt the involvement and complicity of the Pakistani establishment in this misadventure. It raises serious doubts about the professed aim of 'defusing tension' as averred by Foreign Minister Sartaj Aziz. The evidence will also establish that the management of this enterprise is in the hands of those who put it in place in the first instance. It raises doubts about the brief that Minister Aziz carries, and at whose dictates he is actually working.

The making public of this evidence, at this juncture, is to expose the Pakistani game plan to the entire world; to pre-empt any designs that Pakistan may be nurturing about obscuring the central issue of their involvement, complicity, and continued support to an armed intrusion and aggression in which Pakistani regular troops are participating; to defeat, in advance, the Pakistani aim of dangerously attempting to reopen the sensitive and settled issue of the line of control; and above all, to re-emphasise and reassert the Indian position. There is only one aspect of this Pakistani misadventure that can be discussed: earliest restoration of the *status quo ante*, and reaffirmation of the inviolability of the line of control. This is the very minimum imperative for the maintenance of peace and security in the region.

Ladies and gentlemen, I will now ask that two recorded conversations between the chief of army staff of the Pakistani Army and his chief of the general staff be played. The first conversation took place on 26 May, the second on 29 May. The transcripts of these conversations will be distributed simultaneously.

Transcripts of conversations between Lt Gen Mohammad Aziz, Chief of General Staff and Gen Pervez Musharraf, Chief of Army Staff, Pakistan.

Aziz spoke from Pakistan to Musharraf who was on a visit to China.
Pakistan: Lt Gen Mohd Aziz, Chief of General Staff
China: Gen Pervez Musharraf, Chief of Army Staff
First recording: 26 May

AZIZ: How is the visit going?

MUSHARRAF: Yes, very well, okay. And what else is the news on that side?

AZIZ: Ham-dul-ullah. There is no change on the ground situation. They have started rocketing and strafing. That has been upgraded a little. It has happened yesterday also and today. Today, high altitude bombing has been done.

MUSHARRAF: On their side in those positions?

AZIZ: In those positions, but in today's bombing, about three bombs landed on our side of the line of control. No damage, sir.

MUSHARRAF: Is it quite a lot?

AZIZ: Sir, about 12–13 bombs were dropped from which three fell on our side, which does not appear to be a result of inaccuracy. In my interpretation, it is a sort of giving of a message that if need be, we can do it on the other side as well. It is quite distance apart. Where the bombs have been dropped, they have tried to drop from a good position where they are in difficulty, from behind the LOC, but they have fallen on our side of the LOC. So I have spoken to the foreign secretary, and I have told him that he should make the appropriate noises about this in the press.

MUSHARRAF: They (Indians) should also be told.

AZIZ: That we have told, foreign secretary will also say and Rashid will also say. He will not, generally speaking, make any such mistake about those other bombs falling on the other side. Our stand should be that all these bombs are falling on our side. We will not come into that situation. The guideline that they have given, we have stressed that we should say that this build-up and employment of air strike, which has been done under the garb of us (?). Actually, they are targetting our position on the LOC and our logistic build-up. These, possibly, they are taking under the garb having intention for operation the craft (?) line of control and this need to be taken note of and we would retaliate in kind is what happened? So the entire build-up we want to give this colour.

MUSHARRAF: Absolutely okay. Yes, this is better. After that, has there been any talk with them? Any meetings, etc.?

AZIZ: Yesterday, again, in the evening.

MUSHARRAF: Who all were there?

AZIZ: Actually, we insisted that a meeting should be held because otherwise that friend of ours, the incumbent of my old chair, we thought lest he give some interpretation of his own. We should do something ourselves by going there.

MUSHARRAF: Was he little disturbed? I heard that there was some trouble in Sialkot.

AZIZ: Yes, there was one in Daska. On this issue, there was trouble. Yes, he was little disturbed about that, but I told him that such small things keep happening, and we can reply to such things in a better way.

MUSHARRAF: Absolutely.

AZIZ: There is no such thing to worry.

MUSHARRAF: So that briefing to Mian Saheb that we did, was the forum the same as where we had done previously? There at Jamshed's place?

AZIZ: No, in Mian Saheb's office.

MUSHARRAF: Oh, I see. There. What was he saying?

AZIZ: From here, we had gone Choudhary Zafar Saheb, Mehmood, myself, and Tauqir. Because before going, Tauqir had spoken with his counterpart. We carried that tape with us.

MUSHARRAF: So what was he (Indian counterpart) saying?

AZIZ: That is very interesting. When you come, I will play it for you. Its focus was that these infiltrators, who are sitting here, they have your help and artillery support without which they could not have come to J&K. This is not a very friendly act, and it is against the spirit of the Lahore declaration. Then Tauqir told him that if your boys tried to physically attack the line of control and go beyond it and that the bombs were planted on the Turtuk Bridge and the dead body received in the process was returned with military honours. And I said I thought that there was good enough indication you would not enter into this type of misadventure, and all this build-up that you are doing, one or more brigade strength and fifty to sixty aircraft are being collected. These are excuses for undertaking some operations against the various spaces, so I had put him on the defensive. Then he said the same old story. He would put three points again and again that they (militants) should not be supported. And without your support, they could not be there. They have sophisticated weapons, and we will flush them out. We will not let them stay there. But this is not a friendly act.

MUSHARRAF: So did they talk of coming out and meeting somewhere?

AZIZ: No, no, they did not.

MUSHARRAF: Was there some other talk of putting pressure on us?

AZIZ: No. He only said that they (militants) will be given suitable reception. This term he used. He said they will be flushed out, and every time Tauqir said that please tell us some detail. Detail about how many have gone into your area, what is happening there? Then I will ask the concerned people, and then we will get back to you. So whenever he asked these details, he would say we will talk about this when we meet, then I will give details. This means they are possibly looking forward to the next round of talks, in which the two sides could meet. This could be the next round of talks between the two PMs, which they are expecting it. Sir, very good thing, no problem.

MUSHARRAF: So, many times we had discussed, taken your (PM's?) blessings and yesterday also I told him that the door of discussion, dialogue must be kept open and rest, no change in ground situation.

AZIZ: So no one was in a particularly disturbed frame of mind.

MUSHARRAF: Even your seat man?

AZIZ: Yes, he was disturbed. Also, Malik Saheb was disturbed, as they had been even earlier. Those two's views were that the status quo and the present position of Gen Hassan (?). No change should be recommended in that. But he was also saying that any escalation after that should be regulated, as there may be the danger of war. On this logic, we gave the suggestion that there was no such fear as the scruff (tooti) of their (militants) neck is in our hands. Whenever you want, we could regulate it. Ch Zafar Saheb coped very well. He gave a very good presentation of our viewpoint. He said we had briefed the PM earlier and given an assessment. After this, we played the tape of Tauqir. Then he said that what we are seeing, that was our assessment, and those very stages of the military situation were being seen, which it would not be a problem for us to handle. Rest, it was for your guidance how to deal with the political and diplomatic aspects. We told him there is no reason of alarm and panic. Then he said that when I came to know seven days back, when corps commanders were told. The entire reason of the success of this operation was this total secrecy. Our experience was that our earlier efforts failed because of lack of secrecy. So the top priority is to accord confidentiality to ensure our success. We should respect this and the advantage we have from this would give us a handle.

MUSHARRAF: Rest (baki), is Mian Saheb okay?

AZIZ: Okay. He was confident just like that, but for the other two. Shamshad as usual was supporting. Today, for the last two hours, the BBC has been continuously reporting on the air strikes by India. Keep using this. Let them keep dropping bombs. As far as internationalisation is concerned, this is the fastest this has happened. You may have seen in the press about UN Secretary General Kofi Annan's appeal that both countries should sit and talk.

Second recording, 29 May

AZIZ: This Is Pakistan. Give me Room No. 83315 (same room number). Hello.

MUSHARRAF: Hello, Aziz.

AZIZ: The situation on ground is okay, no change. This area, but it is not brought down by attack. One of their MI-17 arms (?) was brought down. Further, the position is we had approached to our position. It was brought down. Rest is okay. Nothing else except there is a development. Have you listened to yesterday's news regarding Mian Saheb speaking to his counterpart? He told him that the spirit of Lahore Declaration and escalation has been done by your people. Specially wanted to speak to me thereafter. He told Indian PM that they should have waited instead of upping the ante by using air force and all other means. He (Nawaz) told him (Indian PM) that he suggested Sartaj Aziz could go to New Delhi to explore the possibility of defusing the tension.

MUSHARRAF: Okay.

AZIZ: Which is likely to take place, most probably, tomorrow.

MUSHARRAF: Okay.

AZIZ: Our other friend (Lt Gen Ziauddin, DG ISI, or it could be the United States) might have also put pressure on. For that, today they will have a discussion at foreign office about 9.30 and Zafar Saheb (Lt Gen Saeeduz Zaman Zafar, GOC 11 Corps and acting chief) is supposed to attend.

MUSHARRAF: Okay.

AZIZ: Aziz Saheb (Sartaj Aziz, foreign minister) has discussed with me, and my recommendation is that dialogue option is always open. But in their first meeting, they must give no understanding or no commitment on ground situation.

MUSHARRAF: Very correct. You or Mehmood (GOC X Corps, Rawalpindi) must have to go with Zafar because they don't know about the ground situation.

AZIZ: This week, we are getting together at 8 o'clock because meeting will be at 9.30, so Zafar Saheb will deliberate it. We want to suggest to Zafar that they have to maintain that they will not be talking about ground situation. All that you say. So far, as the ground situation is concerned. Subsequently, DGMOs can discuss with each other and work out the modus operandi.

MUSHARRAF: Idea on LOC

AZIZ: Yes. Hint is that given that the LOC has many areas where the interpretation of either side is not what the other side believes. So comprehensive deliberation is required. So that can be worked out by DGMOs.

MUSHARRAF: If they are assured that we are here from a long period. We have been sitting here for long. Like in the beginning, the matter is the same. No post was attacked, and no post was captured. The situation is that we are along our defensive line of control. If it is not in his (Sartaj Aziz's) knowledge, then discuss it altogether. Emphasise that for years, we are here only.

MUSHARRAF: Yes, this point should be raised. We are sitting on the same LOC since a long period.

AZIZ: This is their weakness. They are not agreed on the demarcation under UN's verification, whereas we are agreed. We want to exploit it.

MUSHARRAF: This is in Simla Agreement that we cannot go for UN intervention.

AZIZ: Our neighbour does not accept their presence or UNMOGIP arrangement for survey for the area. So we can start from the top, from 9842 (NJ 9842). On this line, we can give them logic, but in short, the recommendation for Sartaj Aziz Saheb is that he should make no commitment in the first meeting on military situation. And he should not even accept ceasefire because if there is ceasefire, then vehicles will be moving (on Dras–Kargil highway). In this regard, they have to use their own argument that whatever is interfering with you. That we don't know, but there is no justification about tension on LOC. No justification. We want to give them this type of brief, so that he does not get into any specifics.

MUSHARRAF: All right.

AZIZ: In this connection, we want your approval and what is your programme?

MUSHARRAF: I will come tomorrow. We are just leaving within an hour. We are going to Shenzhen. From there, by evening, we will be in Hong Kong. There will be a flight tomorrow from Hong Kong, so we will be there at Lahore in the evening via Bangkok flight.

AZIZ: Sunday evening, you will be at Lahore. We will also indicate that if there is more critical situation, then it (Sartaj visit) should be deferred for another day or two. We can discuss on Monday and then do.

MUSHARRAF: Has this MI-17 not fallen in our area?

AZIZ: No, sir. This has fallen in their area. We have not claimed it. We have got it claimed through the mujahideen.

MUSHARRAF: Well done.

AZIZ: But top wise side, crashing straight before our eyes.

MUSHARRAF: Very good. Now, are they facing any greater difficulty in flying them? Are they scared or not? This also you should note. Are they coming any less nearer?

AZIZ: Yes, there is a lot of pressure on them. They were talking about greater air defence than they had anticipated. They can't afford to lose any more aircraft. There has been less intensity of air flying after that.

MUSHARRAF: Very good, first class. Is there any build up on the ground?

AZIZ: Just like that, but the movement is pretty sluggish and slow. One or two are coming near number six. Till now, only one call sign in which one has not reached the valley so far. Now, the air people and the ground people will stay back, and then the situation will be okay.

MUSHARRAF: See you in the evening.

It was very much clear that Pakistan's regular army made intrusions in our territory and provoking India for a war, which can be lead into full-fledge war between two countries and affect the peace of Asia. This made world countries, their leaders, and think tanks to take a clear stand against Pakistan.

Bruce Riedel was Special Assistant to the President and Senior Director for Near East and South Asia Affairs in the National Security Council at the White House from 1997 to 2001, wrote in *American Diplomacy and 1999 Kargil Summit at Blair House* that, 'In the winter of 1999, however, Pakistani backed Kashmir militants, and regular army units moved early into evacuated positions of the Indians, cheating on the tradition. The Pakistani backed forces, thus gained a significant tactical advantage over the only ground supply route Indian forces can use to bring in supplies to the most remote eastern third of Kashmir. By advancing onto these mountaintops over looking the Kargil highway, Pakistan was threatening to weaken Indian control over a significant part of the contested province.'

This shows clear-cut view of US on the issue. Other western countries, as well as many Asian countries, also took PRO-INDIAN stance publicly.

This was perhaps the first time in many years when we were not on diplomatic defensive over Kashmir in front of world.

International support on issue was immense in favour of India and against Pakistan. On other hand, Pakistan lost credibility in front of world. Its so-called promises: agreements efforts of keeping peace in subcontinent were totally exposed. Pakistan was standing as culprit in front of world leadership.

The United States condemned Pakistan's 'infiltration of armed intruders', and went public with information that most of the seven hundred men who had crossed the line of control were attached to the Pakistani Army's 10th Corps. [4]

France and Russia also came out with strong statements of support to India. China and Britain expressed their concern over the conflict, and believed it should be sorted out bilaterally. Prime Minister Atal Bihari Vajpayee gave his hard impressions by rejecting UN Secretary-General Kofi Annan's offer of an envoy for negotiating peace.

The Pakistanis were surprised by the US and other nation's position. Pakistan always assumed that US would always back them against India. This was a major diplomatic setback to Pakistan.

Diplomatically, Pakistan was on the defensive. Militarily, Pakistan did not really expect India's tough response, and has been forced to rethink and regret its strategy at Kargil. By the last week of June, Pakistan was loosing its grip over occupied land in Kargil, and their casualties were increasing. This made Pakistan feel trapped very badly.

In late June, Clinton called Nawaz Sharif to stress that the United States saw Pakistan as the aggressors, and to reject the fiction that the fighters were the separatist guerrillas. He sent Tony Zinni, the marine general in charge of the US central command, to reinforce the message in person to Musharraf and Nawaz Sharif. Tony warned Musharraf that India would cross the line of control itself if Pakistan did not pull back.[7]

Nawaz Sharif became very desperate, as he saw Pakistan getting isolated on the issue in the front of world. He urgently requested American intervention to stop the Indian counter-attack. Washington was clear. The solution required a Pakistani withdrawal behind the LOC, nothing else would do. In the last days of June, Sharif began to ask to see President Clinton directly to plead his case. On 2 July, Nawaz again asked US president for help. US told him about which India was very much adamant 'back off from our land'.

On the third, Sharif was more desperate and told the US President Clinton he was ready to come immediately to Washington to seek their help. The president repeated his caution. Come only if you are ready to withdraw. I can't help you if you are not ready to pull back. He urged Sharif to consider carefully the wisdom of a trip to Washington under these constraints. Sharif said he was coming and would be there on the fourth.[8]

'This guy's coming literally on a wing and a prayer,' said the president. 'That's right,' said Bruce Riedel.[9]

On 4 July, Nawaz met Clinton. Clinton literally went bully on Nawaz, and almost threatened him to give a joint statement (see Appendix VII, Joint Statement of Nawaz Sharif and US President Clinton at Blair House on withdrawal of Pakistan Army, 4 July 1999) immediately for withdraw of his force.

Nawaz and Pakistan Army leadership got trapped badly in Indian diplomatic cyclone, broke out, issued a joint statement to withdraw its forces and to respect the LOC as per Shimla Agreement.

India's diplomatic, military, and political response on Kargil was brilliant example of coronations between civil and army leadership. On other hand, Pakistan's civil-military conflict widened. Nawaz and Musharraf both blamed each other for Kargil defeat, relations between them got more bitter, and resulted in one more military coup.

Pakistan Foreign Minister Sarrtaj Aziz Arrives In New Delhi June 12, 1999 For Talks with The Indian External Affairs Minister Jaswant Singh.

References :-

1. Gourav Swanat, *Dateline Kargil*
2. Raj Chengappa, *Advantage India,* Article published in India Today, 14 June 1999
3. Jaswant Singh, *In Service of Emergent India*
4. Strobe Tallbot, *The Day A Nuclear Conflict Was Averted*
5. China urges Pakistan, India to respect LOC, News International, 2 July 1999
6. Russia rejects Pakistan Version of Kargil Crisis, The Hindu, 2 July
7. *Engaging India: Diplomacy, Democracy, and the Bomb by Strobe Talbott*
8. Bruce Riedel, *American Diplomacy and the 1999 Kargil Summit at Blair House*
9. Strobe Tallbot, *The Day A Nuclear Conflict Was Averted*

CHAPTER 15

WHY PAKISTAN DID IT?

Leadership is a privilege to better the lives of others. It is not an opportunity to satisfy personal greed.

- Mwai Kibaki, Former President of Kenya

CHAPTER 15

What are the motives and plans of Pakistan establishment behind Kargil Operation? Why Pakistan Army and Government wanted to jeopardise peace process between both countries? So why did they do it?

It was not the first time that Pakistan Army planned this type of operation against India. In 1947, they did—under facade of tribals—and made an attempt to seize Kashmir from us. Then in May 1965, Pakistan launched a 'feeler' in the Rann of Kutch; firstly, to test the waters and tried to estimate whether India had the political will to respond to a military operation, and to test the effectiveness and efficiency of its newly acquired weapons from US.

After four months of border skirmishes, Pakistan undertook its second military misadventure to wrest Jammu and Kashmir forcibly. In August/ September 1965, Pakistan made a large-scale infiltration of its army regulars into the Kashmir Valley to create insurgency. Believing the Muslims of Jammu and Kashmir would revolt against India with their little help. Pakistan launched Operation Gibraltar, a plan to provoke uprisings in Jammu and Kashmir by infiltrating military commandos under facade of 'Mujahidins' to conduct sabotage and prod the Kashmiri people against Indian forces, but failed and beaten back.

This was followed by Operation Grand Slam, an aggression in the Chamb sector of Jammu to capture the strategic border town of Akhnoor, and to cut the communications to our troops deployed in south of Pir Panjal. In a bold policy decision, Indian Prime Minister, Lal Bahadur Shastri, gave the clearance for the army to cross the international border and open a second front in Punjab. The Indian response to cross the international border was unexpected by Pakistan; and after a series of hard-fought battle, a ceasefire was declared on 23 September, thus, ending the second Indo-Pakistan War.

The Kargil plan was not an on the spot creation. It was planned much in advance, and resources for it were catered for. The plan was a part of operation TOPAC engineered by Gen Zia.

Operation Tupac (or Topac) is the existing code name of an ongoing Cold War Military Intelligence Contingency Program run by the Pakistan Inter-Service Intelligence (ISI) Agency, active since the 1980s. The program has a three-part action plan for covert support of militancy in Jammu and Kashmir. One, infilterte more foreign terrorist to spred insurgency; two, to make people rebel against Government of India; three, to disturb the secularism peace of region. It was authorised and initiated by order of the President of Pakistan Mohd. Zia Ul Haq, in 1988, after the failure of 'Operation Gibraltar', the main objective of operation Topac is to utilise the spy network to sponsor insurgency and militant activities in Kashmir valley, as well as in other part of India to unstable the sovereignty of it.

The Pakistan Army had also planned the invasion of the Kargil Dras region fourteen years ago. The brain behind this strategy was the then Brigadier Azzizudia (Aziz) who was given charge of a Pakistani brigade in POK in 1985. The shrewd brigadier conceived the invasion plan after intensive tour and study of topography of Pakistan occupied Kashmir. In 1994, he was promoted and sent back to POK as head of northern command. It was the time that he finalised the intrusion plan.

Later in an interview with leader journalist, Veer Sanghvi, former prime minister of Pakistan, Benazir Bhutto, admitted that the Kargil like plan was presented in fornt of her in her regime. She said Pervej Musharraf was also part of presentation team. As Bhutto said, she refused the plan immediately after thinking about its consequences.

Shaukat Qadir has argued that Kargil was the product of a unique confluence of individuals in the Pakistani chain of command, all of whom had something to prove.[1]

Siachin and Kashmir were the main reason for Kargil conflict. Pakistani Army and political regime thought this goal can be achieved through crossing and capturing the heights over the LOC.

Pakistan had the following strategic aims:

1) Pakistan wanted a better bargaining position to negotiate over Siachin by capturing a chunk of Indian land.

2) To seek an international support for the Pakistan's goal on Kashmir issue, especially of Muslim countries, by raising the Kashmir issue as communal.

Pakistan had the following military aims:

1) Cut off the strategic national highway, 1A. By dominating this highway, Pakistan can easily cut the rest of India from northern part of Kashmir, and firmly hold the region by its army dominance over it to disrupt the supplies and reinforcement to Indian troops and base at Siachin.
2) Alter the status of LOC: Pakistan Army and government never wanted the clear line of control. They wanted it to be unstable and unclear to raise conflicts, as well as issue of Kashmir on its platform.
3) Give impetus to insurgency in Kashmir Valley and elsewhere in J&K.

Pakistan Army leadership always thought that all above earlier operation could not reach to the results they wanted because they were not properly executed, instead of believing that India had more bigger and strong army and had a better foreign policy than Pakistan. They always felt that a small right click can damage and destroy India, and in search of that right click, they wanted to turn every stone of possibility.

According to Altaf Gohar, the once powerful information secretary to Ayub Khan in the 1960s, while writing in the Pakistani newspaper, *The nation*, states that all operation against India were conceived and launched on the basis of one assumption; that Indian are too cowardly and ill organised to offer any effective military response, which can cause any threat to Pakistan. The Pakistan military establishment was becoming more frustrated with India's success in containing the military in J and K to within manageable limits. Pakistan's policy and desire to bleed India through a strategy of 'Let the India Bleeding with the Thousand Cuts' was getting slow and effect less.

By the invasion of heights, they wanted their control on Kashmir Valley. They hoped to hold the heights firmly, so they could launch group of infiltrators easily on particular small assignment and could return easily after completing. But they severely underestimated the determined Indian military and diplomatic reaction, the extensive military capability required to defend their over-stretched positions, and the anxious international reaction. The false optimism of the architects of the Kargil intrusion, coloured by the illusion of a cheap victory, was not only the main driver of the operation; and, hence, the crisis. It also was the cause of Pakistan's most damaging military defeat since the loss of East Pakistan in December 1971 (as described by Hasan-Askari Rizvi in book *Asymmetric Warfare in South Asia* and by Altaf Gauhar in *Four Wars, One Assumption*).

The Planning of Kargil Blunder

Initially, the Kargil was planned by Gen. Pervez Musharraf and three of his loyal and trustworthy army commanders, Lt Gen Mohammad Ahmed, Lt Gen Mahmud Aziz, and Major General Javed Hasan only. Even naval and air force chief were not informed at planning level.

While preparation of executing the beginning in November/December 1998, the subject was casually discussed with Prime Minister Nawaz Sharif. Army Chief of Pakistan, Pervez Musharaff, presented a plan. He presented that the Kashmir movement needed a push from Pakistan, and for that, Pakistan needed to infiltrate more Mujahidins in Kashmir. Also presented that Pakistan need to establish few firm based in its own territory (a big lie, not mentioning the plan of crossing of LOC) to support the crossing of Mujahidins in valley, and to provide logistic support for them.

It is significant to note that at this very time, the first reports of Indian Prime Minister Atal Behari Vajpayee's impending Lahore bus visit began to appear in the press. By mid- February, the Pakistani Government, under Nawaz Sharif, found itself on two contradictory tracks with India. Permission to launch a sizeable stealth operation to capture the Kargil heights had been given only weeks before the dramatic Lahore visit by Vajpayee. Even after the Lahore process was under way, Sharif did not reverse the military operation that was then well in motion.[2]

Nawaz Sharif, who was already on targets of orthodox and radical leaders of Pakistan for being so nice and developing the fruits of friendship between both countries, got a chance to settle the score of internal politics by giving it approval without going in details and consequences

Prime Minister Nawaz Sharif visited the town of Skardu in the Northern Areas on 29 January 1999. Sharif's visit seems to indicate that he had been briefed earlier, prompting his decision to go to the FCNA area.[3]

According to Lt Gen Mahmud Ahmed, he personally briefed Sharif during his visit to Skardu. He explained the vulnerabilities and what he suspected the Indians were planning. Sharif replied with a characteristic economy of words, simply telling Mahmud to fix it. A week later, Prime Minister Sharif, again, visited 10 Corps areas on 5 February 1999. This time, he visited the LOC in the 12 division areas at Kel in the Neelum Valley, also located in the Northern Areas of Pakistan. Lt Gen Mahmud, again, briefed the prime minister on developments along the LOC, and in particular explained the Neelum Valley problems.[4]

On seventeenth of May, the army and civil leadership met for the discussion over present LOC situation in a formal Defence Committee of Cabinet (DCC). Nawaz was present in meeting, along with foreign minister, foreign secretary, defence secretary, and principle secretary. DGMO Tauqir Zia provided some details about the military situation, and reportedly said that the aim of the operation was to boost the freedom movement in Kashmir. According to Defence Secretary Iftikhar, after the briefing was over, Lt Gen Aziz then said to the prime minister, 'Sir, it was Quaid-i-Azam and the Muslim league that made Pakistan. Their names are enshrined for all time. Now, your name and your Muslim league will be associated with the liberation of Kashmir and the completion of Pakistan.' Iftikhar said that their remarks made the prime minister feel very good about the whole operation.[5]

Later, when whole episode backfired, Nawaz washed off his hand by denying any information or presentation he received from army leadership on Kargil plan.

Till end of the May, he was being briefed positively on the operation by army top commanders, but at the end of June—when Pakistan started falling from each and every peak in a briefing—Musharraf himself told him without giving any clear view on the real positions (Pakistan Army loosing posts very rapidly) that army can be pulled back only if political leadership wants them to do. Now, this was Pervez Musharraf's turn to wash off his hands on the matter.

Nawaz found himself trapped; later, Pervez Musharraf also found himself totally exposed in summer of 1999 when RAW released a tape (mention in previous chapter) of his and Lt Gen Mohammad Aziz in which he himself exposing all his misadventure and lies he spoke to Nawaz, world, and to his own Pakistan people.

Musharraf, the Culprit

Gen Pervez Musharraf has long standing links with several Islamic fundamentalist groups. The first assignment given by Zia to him was in the training of the mercenaries recruited by various Islamic extremist groups for fighting against the Soviet troops in Afghanistan. It was during those days that Gen Musharraf came into contact with Osama bin Laden, then a reputed civil engineer of Saudi Arabia who had been recruited by the USA's Central Intelligence Agency (CIA) and brought to Pakistan for constructing bunkers for the Afghan Mujahideen in difficult terrain.[6]

Pervez Musharraf always used to show his anger over India's Siachin invasion (that's what he thought), and always discussed the plan to take ravange of Siachin among other officers. In 1987, Pervez was promoted to brigadier. He was personally chosen by then president and chief of army staff, Zia Ul Haq. Gen Zia was again impressed by Pervez for his experience of mountain and arctic warfare. He immediately gave him free hand to plan an attack on Siachin and occupy it.

In September 1987, an assault was launched under the command of Brig Pervez at Bilafond La to recapture the lost height of Siachin. His attempt was beaten back very badly by Indian Army, and that caused Pakistan a loss of over 300 soldiers.

Later in 1998, the same Pervez, who was commissioned as young second lieutant and then became brigadier, was now General of Pakistan Army and known as most shrewd army general and who also later became dictator of Pakistan. After beaten back so many times by Indian Army, still Siachin was on Gen Parvez's top priority. What he could not achieve twelve years before, now he had opportunity and full authority to make a plan to arrest Siachin from India through Kargil.

Initially, the Kargil Operation was known only to Gen Pervez Musharraf; chief of general staff, Lt Gen Mohammad Aziz, FCNA (Force Command Northern Areas); Commander Lt Gen Javed Hassan; and 10 Corps commander, Lt Gen Mahmud Ahmad.

'The majority of corps commanders and principal staff officers were kept in the dark. Even the then director general military operations (DGMO), Lt Gen Tauqir Zia, came to know about it later,' says Gen Shaid Aziz in his interview in a Pakistan newspaper *Dawn*. He also confirmed, 'There were no Mujahideen, only taped wireless messages, which fooled no one. Our soldiers were made to occupy barren ridges with handheld weapons and ammunition.' Aziz, at the time, was serving as director general of the analysis wing of Inter-Services Intelligence (ISI).

All previous generals of Pakistan Army had strong views and prejudice about Indian establishment. Musharraf can be ranked on top among of them. He was not in support of any peace dialogue between both countries. At the time of Lahore Summit, he avoided one-to-one interaction with Indian Prime Minister, Mr Atal Bihari Vajpayee, in welcome ceremony at Wagha Border because he didn't want to be seen saluting the head of a country he considered as enemy. By this arrogant, undiplomatic act, one can imagine his odium thoughts and ill feeling toward Indian and its civil and army leadership.

So many times he publicly reflected his hate toward India, and clearly supported the Kashmiri militants. He was the first general of Pakistan Army to demonstrate that it is duty of world's Muslims to support the Jihad against India.

He publicly disregarded the Lahore Declaration signed by Mr Atal Behari Vajpayee and Mr Nawaz Sharif in his speech in April 1998 at a conference in Karachi, just after one month of Lahore Summit.

The captured diary of a Pakistani Captain, Hussain Ahmad of the 12 NLI in Mushkoh sector, tells about views of Musharraf, 'The Diarist calls the intrusion a move to establish a new LOC and quotes Pakistan's COAS, General Pervez Musharraf, who visited the Mushkoh sector on 28 March, describing the gambit as a reply to (India's) Siachen invasion of 1984.' The General handed out Rs 8000 for sweets to be distributed amongst 12 NLI 'Mujahids'.[8]

Musharraf not only betrayed the Lahore Summit, but also betrayed his own military and soldiers. Pakistan Army never accepted the dead bodies of NLI soldiers because they insisted it were 'Mujahidins' who were fighting not Pakistan Army. India gave a decent burial to around 300 to 400 of Pakistanis in our territory with honour and Pakistan flag after being refused from their own army. Indian Army showed a great example of professionalism. Later in his book, Musharraf admitted that around 350 soldiers died on other hand. Nawaz, in his interview, claimed the numbers were more than 4,000. So many Pakistani officers and soldiers are still missing after Kargil War.

The eight Pakistani POWs, held captive during the Kargil conflict, were being released by India as a goodwill gesture.

Did Nawaz Knew about Kargil?

Yes, he was aware, but never thought about the consequences of it. He, himself, wanted to improve his image as 'Pro-Kashmiri' in Pakistan, and finding a good opportunity in Musharraf's plan for this. So more relevant question is why Nawaz approved Kargil like plan?

So what exactly Nawaz Sharif was thinking, and what explains his dual, often contrasting personality? Answers lie not only in his past, but also in the history of Pakistan. This 'disease', if one may call so, after all isn't Sharif specific; but first, let's discuss who the PML-N leader is. Sharif entered politics as a protege of Gen Zia-ul-Haq in 1981. Then at thirty-one, he was a pro-military conservative businessman with grievances against the Zulfikar Ali Bhutto Government, which has nationalised the steel mills owned by Sharif's father. It was, therefore, quite natural for him to carry forward not just the anti-Bhutto outlook, but also the legacy of Zia when he first took over as Pakistan's Prime Minister in 1990. In 1997, when Sharif again came to power, he was hardly different, still pursuing Islamist policies to bolster his position. Thus, he introduced an Islamic *Shariah* bill, reinforcing the Islamisation process initiated by Zia. Sharif had also planned to make further amendments to the constitution, declaring himself *Amirul Mominin* (absolute leader of Muslims).[9]

According to other generals, who later revealed the information, Nawaz Sharif was shown the location of their men and Indian Army, but not the LOC. Sharif, too, believed that if these fighters get Kargil—and later Siachen if not Kashmir—his political stature would rival that of the founder of Pakistan, Mohammed Ali Jinnah himself.

In an interview, Shahid Aziz said that a senior Pakistani officer told that Sharif wanted to know when the Pak Army was 'gifting him Kashmir'. The conversation allegedly happened during a high-level meet between army top brass and Pak Government in Kel (a village and Pakistan Army base opposite side of Kargil sector in POK) just before Kargil War.

In an interview, Musharraf also confirmed Nawaz's visit in Kel. Musharraf held out four photographs showing Sharif's visit to Kel front lines, which took place on 5 February 1999, many days before Vajpayee's visit to Pakistan. 'Look at these pictures,' General Musharraf said. 'In one of these pictures, I am receiving him (Sharif). In another, he is being briefed by Commander Mehmood at Kel who later became DG ISI, while in yet another, he is addressing the troops there. All these pictures were taken the same day.'

'Why had he gone to Kel at a time when all such things were under way? During heavy snow. . . what was the necessity that forced him to go to Kel? One cannot do anything if someone is telling lies so consistently,' Musharraf said. [10]

More or less, Nawaz's basic political agenda is anti-India, and he found himself more comfortable between his voter and army institute by following the same. Jaswant Singh also mentioned about Nawaz's dual character and his political priority over good relations with India in his book, 'We were sitting on adjacent chairs and were both to speak on the merits of democracy and freedom, or some such uplifting theme. We were being hosted by National Endowment for Democracy in honour of the fiftieth anniversary of freedom and democracy in India. We chatted amicably enough in the post–lunch session as the meeting droned on and on. It was than Nawaz Sharif's turn to intervene. He went up to the podium, pulled out a prepared text, and as they say colloquially, "Let India and Jaswant Singh have it". I was more amused than either alarmed or astonished. But I was, I must admit, at least a bit of all three. Upon returning to his chair, Nawaj Sharif, transformed into politeness itself, said, "Sorry, Jaswant ji, I had to say all those things. You know I have to send message back home." I responded, "Do not give it another thought, Nawaz Sharif Sahib. These are the merits and perils of democracy, but you need not to worry because on theme, which I speak, will not even use small arms fire against Pakistan." I don't think he caught on to my use of this somewhat military metaphor. But much later, in different circumstances and both of us were in position of some responsibility in government, I was struck again by how he demonstrated the very same tendency: peace and accord and goodwill during meetings, invective and abuse, even conflict and war afterward. Jaswant Singh writes in his book *In Service of Emergent India*.'

Nawaz Sharif was doing what he was supposed to do as per his political requirements, but it went wrong, and for sure in the way that will lead him to bigger problems.

It is very significant to note that at this very time, the first reports of Indian Prime Minister Atal Behari Vajpayee's impending Lahore bus visit began to appear in the press. By mid-February, the Pakistan, under Nawaz Sharif, found itself on two contradictory tracks with India. Permission to launch a sizeable stealth operation to capture the Kargil heights had been given only weeks before the dramatic Lahore visit by Vajpayee. Even after Lahore process was under way, Sharif did not reverse the military that was then well in motion.[11]

The situation was not comfortable for Nawaz, but he had no other option than let things happen in their own ways—out of his control.

Then happened, Kargil and Sharif found himself on slippery ground. Initially, Sharif championed the cause of Kargil to extract political mileage out of it. But after he was deposed, he took the line that he had no prior information about Kargil. Many experts don't buy this argument. Stephen P. Cohen says, 'Apparently, Sharif decided to give permission for an incursion by the Pakistan military, and either it was larger than he thought it would be or it got to off hands.' The most likely scenario is reconstructed by Prof Samina Yasmeen who argues that Sharif was briefed about the case, but he apparently did not comprehend the nature and possible consequences of adventurism. Maybe he was too much in a hurry to improve his standing within Pakistan to have closely scrutinised the pros and cons of the plan.[12]

Later in an interview, Nawaz said, 'It was a failure because we had hide its objectives and results from our own people and the nation. It had no purpose, no planning, and nobody knows today how many soldiers lost their lives.' He confessed and blamed Musharraf for Kargil blunder.

Five years after the Kargil War, Nawaz Sharif admitted in an interview with Raj Chengappa (*Nawaz Sharif Speaks Out*, India Today, 26 July 2004) that, 'I blundered in making him (Musharraf) army chief.' He also admitted and revealed so many other facts as well on Kargil War in some interview. Same parts of his interview are as follows:

Q. It is now exactly five years since the Kargil War. On 4 July 1999, you flew to the US to seek President Bill Clinton's help in bringing a ceasefire. The US president, in his recent book, talked about that meeting. Why did you go to meet Clinton?

A. I seriously wanted the war to come to an end. Initially, when this scuffle had started, Musharraf said it was the Mujahideen that was fighting in Kashmir. I thought since Mujahideen keep fighting, therefore, it is not a new phenomenon. Later on, I got a call from Vajpayee Saab, saying, 'Nawaz saab, *ye kya ho raha hai?*' I asked, '*Kya ho raha hai?*' Vajpayee said, 'Your army is attacking our army. They are fighting against our army.'

I said there was no Pakistan Army fighting against his army. Vajpayee said, 'Nawaz Saab *aap ko pata nahin hai*? It is your regular forces that are now attacking our positions and have now come into our area. You have occupied our posts.' I said, 'Vajpayee Saab let us find out, and I will investigate the matter.' I suppose I should have known about all this. But frankly, I hadn't been briefed.

Q. So General Musharraf hadn't briefed you of the real intent.
A. No, not at all. He said to me that the Mujahideen are fighting, and the Pakistan Army was not involved.

Q. When did you have this conversation with Vajpayee?
A. Just a couple of days after the incidents. I told Vajpayee Saab that let us tell our respective DGMOs (Directors General of Military Operations) to be in touch and settle the matter. He agreed, but I believe that the conversation the DGMOs had was not a very pleasant one. I feared the matter might get further aggravated. So I called back Vajpayee Saab to request him to instruct his DGMO, and I would do mine so that they could seriously examine the issue. Vajpayee Saab then interrupted me and said, 'Bhai, your forces have attacked our forces, so you should pull them back. There's a great pressure on me to bring our troops out to the other sectors also.'

Q. So what did you do?
A. I thought this matter might become serious, and this might be the beginning of an open war between Pakistan and India. The two nations had just detonated their nuclear bombs, and this would be disastrous. I think Mr Vajpayee also thought it would be very dangerous, and that is why despite being under pressure from his army, he didn't bring his forces on the other sectors of the border.

I kept telling him, 'Let us find a solution.' I sent my foreign minister, Sartaj Aziz, to India. Although reluctant, Mr Vajpayee agreed to receive him. But when he met his counterpart, nothing really happened. Then we were looking for an honourable way to end the battle. Mr Musharraf felt we should bring Mr Clinton into the matter. He pushed me to meet him. Mr Musharraf said, 'Why don't you meet Clinton? Why don't you ask him to bring about a settlement?'

Q. So it was the other way around, and not as General Musharraf had claimed.

A. It was Mr Musharraf who behaved irresponsibly, and it was he who planned the whole affair. Even when I was in Pakistan and in jail, I had said categorically that it was a very confused, ill-planned, and ill-executed affair.

If Mr Vajpayee says that Mr Sharif had stabbed me in the back, I think he is absolutely right. Because he visited Pakistan in February and in May, we were attacking the Indian forces in Kargil, which was absolutely wrong. I hold Mr Musharraf responsible for this. I can only tell Mr Vajpayee that I did not know that I was being stabbed in the back by my own general.

Q. Didn't you ask your army chief what was happening?

A. I didn't approve of this idea from day one. When he committed regular Pakistan forces also to fight the Indian forces, it was a very dangerous development. Mr Musharraf hid all these matters from me. He didn't allow many of these inside developments to reach me.

Q. Do you mean General Musharraf did not brief you at all?

A. Mr Musharraf didn't brief me on any of these things. When Mr Musharraf called his number two from China (where he had paid a visit during the war, a conversation Indian intelligence recorded), Mr Musharraf categorically told him, 'I hope the prime minister is not aware of these things.' He had no authority to start any war against India without the permission of the prime minister, without the permission of the government, without the cabinet's approval.

It was the defence secretary who should have given the permission, the go-ahead signal, to start any move by the army. It happened without all this. A thorough inquiry needs to be conducted in the whole affair. This has been my demand ever since I have been out of power. Lately, General (Antony) Zinni (then chief of US Central Command Forces), who was a close friend of Musharraf, has revealed in his book that it was Mr Musharraf who pushed me to pull out our forces from Kargil.

Q. What are the true figures of the number of Pakistani soldiers killed in the Kargil War?

A. It runs into thousands. The battlefield casualties were more than the combined casualties of the 1965 and 1971 wars. There is no official statement. Some say 2,700, and others say it was more. It was high on both sides.

Q. What was General Musharraf saying during the war?

A. He was telling me that the Mujahideen was taking control of these places. But finally, we came to know that rather than gaining control, they were losing control (laughs).

History and both nation will never forgive Pervez Musharraf for claiming lives of their own, as well as soldiers of India. He will be remembered for his wrongdoing, bad army leadership, and for his notorious dictatorship.

As the debate over Kargil goes on, neither Musharraf nor Sharif is ready to take blame for the Kargil. The task of taking truth out of this blame game is still very difficult for world because that time, there were two power centres in Pkaistan, Nawaz, and Musharaff. Musharraf has all along insisted that all parties involved, including government, were on board. However, Sharif, who was than Prime Minister, insists that he was kept in the dark and that the army top brass had planned the operation on its own. The publication of two books, Nawaz Sherrif's *Ghaddar Koun* (Who is Traitor) and Pervez's *In the Line of Fire* has added only more confusion, with the truth being a major casualty. But history and people of Pakistan should not forgive their culprits. Culprits, who forced their soldiers to illegally occupy another nation's territory, culprits of their own soldiers by denying their dead bodies and not giving the due respect to them and their families, culprits of citizens of Pakistan for telling them lies about event, culprits of so many valuable human lives.

History will never forget Nawaz and Musharaff because of the damage they did and pain gave to the people of subcontinent.

References

1. Shaukat Qadir 'An Analysis of the Kargil Conflict' RUSI Journal (April 2002): 24-30.
2. Feroz Hassan Khan, Peter R Lavoy, Cristopher Clary, Pakistan's motivation and calculations, Asymmetric Warfare in South Asia, Page 86

3. During the Prime Minister's address at Skardu, A discussion of Sharif's visits and briefings can be found in Mazari, The Kargil Conflict 1999,57.

4. Interview with Lt Gen Mahmud Ahmed, 13 January 2004. February 5 is a National holiday in Pakistan marking so called solidarity with the Kashmiris

5. As mentioned By Peter R Levoy, Asymmetric Warfare in South Asia, Page-184

6. B. Raman, in his article GEN. PERVEZ MUSHARRAF : HIS PAST PRESENT & FUTURE

7. G Parthasarathy, Article, This is not Nirvana

8. The Kargil Review Committee Report. Page no. 21

9. HOW SHARIF LET PAKISTAN DOWNSunday, 04 August 2013 | Utpal Kumar

10. SARFARAZ AHMED, HASAN MANSOOR & FARHAN SHARIF, General: Kargil was on before Vajpayee's Lahore visit, Indian Express, July 14,2006

11. (Asymmetric Warfare in South Asia: The Causes and Consequences of the Kargil Conflict :Edited by Peter R. Lavoy)

12. HOW SHARIF LET PAKISTAN DOWN Sunday, 04 August 2013 | Utpal Kumar

CHAPTER 16

WAR HERO

'When you go home, tell them of us;
and say, for your tomorrow, we gave our today.'

I dedicate this chapter to those unsung heroes of our forces who fought for our country and sacrificed their lives in line of duty without getting noticed. They are my heroes as equal as these gallantry awardees.

Capt. Vikram Batra PVC (Posthumous)

Gnr. Yogender Singh Yadav PVC

Lt. Manoj Kumar Pandey
PVC (Posthumous)

Rfn. Sanjay Kumar PVC
(Posthumous)

CHAPTER 16

GALLANTRY AWARDS FOR OPERATION VIJAY

PARAM VIR CHAKRA

1. IC-56959 LT MANOJ KUMAR PANDAY, 1/11 GR (POSTHUMOUS)
2. IC-57556 CAPT VIKRAM BATRA, 13 JAK RIF (POSTHUMOUS)
3. 13760533 RFN SANJAY KUMAR, 13 JAK RIF
4. 2690572 GDR YOGENDER SINGH YADAV, 18 GDRS

MAHAVIR CHAKRA

1. IC-45952 MAJ SONAM WANGCHUK, LADAKH SCOUTS (Indus Wing)
2. IC-51152 MAJ VIVEK GUPTA, 2 RAJ RIF (POSTHUMOUS)
3. IC-52574 MAJ RAJESH SINGH ADHIKARI, 18 GDRS (POSTHUMOUS)
4. IC-55072 MAJ PADMAPANI ACHARYA, 2 RAJ RIF (POSTHUMOUS)
5. IC-57111 CAPT ANUJ NAYYAR, 17 JAT(POSTHUMOUS)

6. IC-58396 CAPT NEIKEZHAKUO KENGURUSE, 2 RAJ (POSTHUMOUS)
7. SS-37111 LT KEISHING CLIFFORD NONGRUM, 12 JAK LI (POSTHUMOUS)
8. SS-37691 LT BALWAN SINGH, 18 GDRS
9. 2883178 NK DIGENDRA KUMAR, 2 RAJ RIF

VIR CHAKRA

1. IC-35204 COL UMESH SINGH BAWA, 17 JAT
2. IC-37020 COL LALIT RAI, 1/11 GR
3. IC-38662 COL MB RAVINDRANATH, 2 RAJ RIF
4. IC-39584 LT COL R VISHWANATHAN, 18 GDRS (POSTHUMOUS)
5. IC-40500 LT COL YOGESH KUMAR JOSHI, 13 JAK RIF
6. IC-43258 MAJ VIJAY BHASKAR, 13 JAK RIF
7. IC-44616 MAJ DEEPAK RAMPAL, 17 JAT
8. IC-47825 MAJ VIKASH VOHRA, 13 JAK RIF
9. IC-48654 MAJ AMRINDER SINGH KASANA, 47 FD REGT
10. IC-52837 MAJ RAJESH SAH, 18 GARH RIF
11. IC-53595 MAJ MOHI SAXENA, 2 RAJ RIF
12. SS-36288 MAJ M SARAVANAN, 1 BIHAR (POSTHUMOUS)
13. IC-53264 CAPT SHAYAMAL SINHA, 27 RAJ
14. IC-54065 CAPT AMOL KALIYA, 12 I (POSTHUMOUS)
15. IC-57021 CAPT SACHIN ANNARAO NIMBALKAR, 18 GDRS
16. IC-57027 CAPT SANJEEV SINGH, ASC, 13 JAK RIF
17. IC-57260 CAPT HANEEF UDDIN, 11 RAJ RIF (POSTHUMOUS)
18. IC-58154 CAPT SUMEET ROY, 18 GARH RIFLES (POSTHUMOUS)
19. IC-58278 CAPT VIJAYANT THAPAR, 2 RAJ RIF (POSTHUMOUS)
20. IC-58564 CAPT MARIDHYODAN VEETIL SOORAJ, 18 GARH RIFLES
21. SS-36261 CAPT JINTU GOGOI, 17 GARH RIF (POSTHUMOUS)
22. SS-37033 CAPT R JERY PREMRAJ, 158 MED REGT (POSTHUMOUS)
23. JC-183573 SUB CHHERING STOBDAN, LADAKH SCOUTS (IW)

24. JC-203851 SUB BAHADUR SINGH, 12 JAK LI (POSTHUMOUS)
25. JC-221082 SUB LOBZANG CHHOTAK LADAKH SCOUTS (IW) (POSTHUMOUS)
26. JC-448357 SUB RANDHIR SINGH, 18 GDRS (POSTHUMOUS)
27. JC-468356 SUB BHAWAR LAL, 2 RAJ RIF (POSTHUMOUS)
28. JC-578216 SUB RAGHUNATH SINGH, 13 JAK RIF
29. JC-468659 NB SUB MANGEJ SINGH, 11 RAJ RIF (POSTHUMOUS)
30. JC-498695 NC SUB KARNAIL SINGH, 8 SIKH (POSTHUMOUS)
31. 2874399 CHM YASHVIR SINGH, 2 RAJ RIF (POSTHUMOUS)
32. 2669264 HAV UDHAM SINGH, 18 GDRS (POSTHUMOUS)
33. 2670242 HAV MADAN LAL, 18 GDRS (POSTHUMOUS)
34. 2874737 HAV SULTAN SINGH NARWARIA 2 RAJ RIF (POSTHUMOUS)
35. 3169696 HAV KUMAR SINGH, 17 JAT (POSTHUMOUS)
36. 3172590 HAV SIS RAM GILL, 8 JAT (POSTHUMOUS)
37. 4180458 HAV JOGINDER SINGH, KUMAON, 27 RAJPUT
38. 9923125 HAV TSEWANG RIGZIN LADAKH SCOUTS (IW) (POSTHUMOUS)
39. 8031499 L/HAV RAM KUMAR, 18 GDRS (POSTHUMOUS)
40. 4067027 NK KASHMIR SINGH, 18 GARH RIF (POSTHUMOUS)
41. 4268024 NK GANESH PRASAD YADAV, 1 BIHAR (POSTHUMOUS)
42. 13745002 NK DEV PARKASH, 13 JAK RIF
43. 9094874 L/NK GH MOHD KHAN, 12 JAK LI (POSTHUMOUS)
44. 14701938 L/NK KHUSHIMAN GURUNG, 1 NAGA
45. 3392872 SEP SATPAL SINGH, 8 SIKH
46. 9924604 SEP TSERING DORJAY, LADAK SCOUTS (IW)
47. 14702837 SEP K ASHULI, 1 NAGA (POSTHUMOUS)
48. 2892944 REN JAI RAM SINGH, 2 RAJ RIF
49. 4075503 RFN ANUSUYA PRASAD, 8 GARH RIF, (POSTHUMOUS)
50. 4075870 RFN KULDEEP SINGH, 18 GARH RIF (POSTHUMOUS)
51. 13758323 RFN SHYAM SINGH, 13 JAK RIF (POSTHUMOUS)
52. 13759408 RFN MEHAR SINGH, 13 JAK RIF

53. 15119305 GNR SANJEEV GOPALA PILLAI ARTY, 4 FD REGT (POSTHUMOUS)
54. WG CDR ANIL KUMAR SINHA (16074) FLYING PILOT
55. SQN LDR AJAY AHUJA (17864) FLYING PILOT (POSTHUMOUS)

SARVOTTAM YUDDH SEVA MEDAL

1. AIR MARSHAL VINOD PATNEY, PVSM, AVSM, Vr. C (6125) FLYING PILOT

UTTAM YUDDHA SEVA MEDAL
2. IC-14039 LT GEN KISHAN PAL, PVSM, VSM, INFANTRY
3. IC-16907 MAJ GEN MOHINDER PURI, INFANTRY
4. IC-24006 BRIG PRAKASH CHAND KATOCH, SC, INFANTRY
5. IC-24255 BRIG AMAR NATH AUL, INFANTRY
6. AVM SATINDER SINGH DHILLON, AVSM, VSM (7980) AERONAUTICAL ENGINEERING (MECHANICAL)
7. AVM JAGNANDAN KUMAR PATHANIA, AVSM, VSM (8053) ADMINISTRATION
8. AVM NARAYAN MENON, AVSM (9005) FLYING PILOY

YUDH SEVA MEDAL

1. IC-19063 BRIG LAKHWINDER SINGH, ARTILLERY
2. IC-23322 BRIG RAMESH KUMAR KAKAR, INFANTRY
3. GO CAPT MATHEWS KURRHIKOMBIL JOSEPH (13393) FLYING PILOT
4. GP CAPT ARVIND RAMACHANDRA OAK (14103) FLYING PILOT
5. WG CDR SUNDERRAMAN NEELAKANTAN, VM (15184) FLYING PILOT
6. WG CDR BIRENDER SINGH DHANOA, VM (15405) FLYING PILOT
7. WG CDR SANDIP SUD (15685) FLYING PILOT
8. WG CDR SANDEEP CHHABRRA (16032) FLYING PILOT

BAR TO SENA MEDAL (GALLANTRY)

1. IC-34600 COL SAMIR KUMAR CHAKRAVORTY, SC, SM, 18 GARH RIF

SENA MEDAL (GALLANTRY)

2. IC-25068 COL DEVENDRA SINGH YADAV, ARMY AVN 663 R & O SQN
3. IC-34423 COL ALOK DEB, ARTY, 197 FD REGT
4. IC-36955 COL PRABHAT RANJAN, ARTY, 108 MED REGT
5. IC-37050 LT COL GIRISH KUMAR MEDIRATTA, ARTY, 1889 LIGHT REGT
6. IC-39611 MAJ SURESH KUMAR JOSHI, 18 GARH RIF
7. IC-41803 MAJ AMBROSE XAVIER AMALARAJ, ARTY, 108 MED REGT
8. IC-47298 MAJ RAVINDRA SINGH, 8 SIKH
9. IC-50074 MAJ GURJEET SINGH, PUNJAB, 5 VIKAS
10. IC-50587 MAJ GURPREET SINGH, 13 JAK RIF
11. IC-51498 MAJ AMITABH ROY, ARTY, 8 SIKH
12. IC-53288 MAJ NAVDEEP SINGH CHEEMA, 27 RAJPUT
13. SS-36635 MAJ AJAY SINGH JASROTIA 13 JAK RIF (POSTHUMOUS)
14. SS-36699 MAJ JOY DASGUPTA, 18 GDRS
15. IC-46723 CAPT HARBIR SINGH, SIKH LI, 5 VIKAS
16. IC-50475 CAPT GANESG BHAT, ARTY, 1889 LIGHT REGT
17. IC-50609 CAPT KAMATH PRASHANT NARAYAN, 1889 LT REGT
18. IC-54099 CAPT MRIDUL KUMAR SINGH, ARTY, 197 FD REGT
19. IC-54362 CAPT P V VIKRAM, ARTY, 141 FD REGT (POSTHUMOUS)
20. IC-58579 CAPT NAVEEN ANABERU NAGAPPA, EME, 13 JAK RIF
21. SS-36929 CAPT SAJU CHERIAN, ARTY, 307 MED REGT
22. SS-36937 CAPT AMIT SHARMA, ARTY, 197 FD REGT
23. MR-7029 CAPT SOMNATH BASU, AMC, 408 FD AMB
24. IC-57422 LT SANJAY BARSHILIA, ARTY, 286 MED REGT

25. IC-58420 LT PRAVEEN TOMAR, ASC, 2 RAJ RIF
26. IC-58520 LT RAKESH KUMAR SEHRAWAT, 8 SIKH
27. SS-37818 LT KANDA BHATTACHARYA, AOC, 8 SIKH (POSTHUMOUS)
28. JC-155752 SUB A HENI MAO, 1 NAGA
29. JC-212589 SUB SUMER SINGH RATHORE, 2 RAJ RIF (POSTHUMOUS)
30. JC-220978 SUB JOGINDER SINGH, 8 SIKH (POSTHUMOUS)
31. JC-488240 SUB SURENDER SINGH, 18 GARH RIF
32. JC-578244 SUB ROMESH CHAND, 13 JAK RIF
33. JC-448592 NB SUB CHANDA JAT, 18 GDRS
34. JC-448733 NB SUB LAL SINGH, 18 GDRS (POSTHUMOUS)
35. JC-468641 NB SUB SUNAYAK SINGH, 2 RAJ RIF
36. JC-588008 NB SUB TUNDUP DORJE, LADAKH SCOUTS (IW)
37. 2871708 HAV SHRI BHAGWAN, 2 RAJ RIF
38. 2876486 HAV RANBIR SINGH, 2 RAJ RIF
39. 2877691 HAV SARMAN SINGH SENGA 2 RAJ RIF (POSTHUMOUS)
40. 3169828 HAV HARI OM, 17 JAT (POSTHUMOUS)
41. 9922696 HAV GHULAM QADIR, LADAKH SCOUTS (IW)
42. 14700648 HAV TAM BAHADUR CHHETRI 1 NAGA (POSTHUMOUS)
43. 2675828 L/HAV RAMESH CHANDRA, 18 GDRS
44. 2679002 NK NIRMAL SINGH YADAV, 18 GDRS
45. 2681582 NK SAMUNDER SINGH, 18 GDRS (POSTHUMOUS)
46. 2681935 NK RAVI KARAN SINGH, 18 GDRS (POSTHUMOUS)
47. 2882280 NK KARANBIR, 2 RAJ RIF
48. 3172785 NK BALWAN SINGH, 17 JAT (POSTHUMOUS)
49. 3388978 NK BAHADUR SINGH, 8 SIKH (POSTHUMOUS)
50. 3389457 NK RANJIT SINGH, 8 SIKH (POSTHUMOUS)
51. 406290 NK JAGAT SINGH, 18 GARH RIF (POSTHUMOUS)
52. 9923077 NK TASHI NURBOO, LADAKH SCOUTS (IW)
53. 13744950 NK MOHAN LAL, 13 JAK RIF
54. 13746128 NK SWARAN SINGH, 13 JAK RIF
55. 2681263 L/NK RAJENDRA KUMAR YADAV 18 GDRS (POSTHUMOUS)

56. 2682054 L/NK SHAKTI SINGH, 18 GDRS
57. 2883917 L/NK NARAYAN SINGH, 2 RAJ RIF
58. 2988446 L/NK BHAGWAN SINGH, 27 RAJPUT (POSTHUMOUS)
59. 4265919 L/NK KISHAN SINGH, 18 GARH RIF (POSTHUMOUS)
60. 4266649 L/NK SURMAN SINGH, 18 GARH RIF (POSTHUMOUS)
61. 13752268 L/NK SARWAN SINGH, 13 JAK RIF
62. 13752567 L/NK KOSHAL KUMAR SHARMA, 13 JAK RIF
63. 13753150 L/NK HARISH PAL, 13 JAK RIF (POSTHUMOUS)
64. 2996629 SEP BHANWAR SINGH INDIA, 27 RAJPUT (POSTHUMOUS)
65. 3188347 SEP SURENDER, 17 JAT (POSTHUMOUS)
66. 3188797 SEP PUNA RAM, 17 JAT
67. 3396374 SEP MAJOR SINGH, 8 SIKH (POSTHUMOUS)
68. 3183340 RFN NARPAL SINGH, 18 GARH RIF (POSTHUMOUS)
69. 4071232 RFN DABAL SINGH, 18 GARH RIF (POSTHUMOUS)
70. 13760079 RFN NATINDER SINGH, 13 JAK RIF
71. 13760224 RFN AJAY PATHANIA, 13 JAK RIF
72. 13761917 RFN SUNIL KUMAR, 13 JAK RIF
73. 13762125 RFN KEWAL KUMAR, 13 JAK RIF
74. 2683467 GDR MUNISH KUMAR, 18 GDRS (POSTHUMOUS)
75. 2683639 GDR KAKYAN SINGH, 18 GDRS
76. 2683738 GDR PRAVIN KUMAR, 18 GDRS (POSTHUMOUS)
77. 2686890 GDR RAJ KUMAR, 18 GDRS (POSTHUMOUS)
78. 2689961 GDR UDHYMAN SINGH, 18 GDRS (POSTHUMOUS)
79. 2690089 GDR DALIP SINGH, 18 GDRS
80. 14404805 GNR JAGADISH PRASAD GUPTA, 286 MED REGT
81. 15312696 SPR M JAYAVEJU, 2 ENGR REGT (POSTHUMOUS)
82. 15398246 SIGMN VINOD KUMAR, 8 MDSR, (POSTHUMOUS)
83. 57867 COY LDR CHHOMBE, 5 VIKAS
84. 61614 ASST LDR TASHI PHONTSOK, 5 VIKAS

VAYU SENA MEDAL (GALLANTRY)

1. GP CAPT SATISH PAL SINGH (13770) FLYING PILOT
2. WG CDR RAGHUNATH NAMBIAR (16378) FLAYING PILOT

3. SQN LDR RAJIV PUNDIR (17143) FLYING PILOT (POSTHUMOUS)
4. SQN LDR MOHAN RAO (17343) FLYING PILOT
5. SQN LDR VISHWAS GAUR (17361) FLYING PILOT
6. SQN LDR SANJAY BHATNAGAR (17363) FLYING PILOT
7. SQN LDR GURCHARAN SINGH BEDI (17448) FLYING PILOY
8. SQN LDR DILIP KUMAR PATNAIK (17464) FLYING PILOT
9. SQN LDR AJAI PRAKASH SRIVASTAVA YSM (17471) FLYING PILOT
10. SQN LDR ALOK CHOUDHARY (18271) FLYING PILOT
11. SQN LDR NARENDER SINGH VERMA (18298) FLYING PILOT
12. SQN LDR AMANJIT SINGH HEER (19521) FLYING PILOT
13. SQN LDR NITISH KUMAR (19898) FLYING PILOT
14. SQN LDR HARENDRA PAL SINGH (20477) FLYING PILOT
15. FLT LT SHREEPED TOKEKAR (21815) FLYING PILOT
16. FIT LT RAJESH WALIA (21858) FLYING PILOT
17. FIT LT ASHISH GUPTA (22121) FLYING PILOY
18. FIT LT SUBRAMANIAM MUHILAN (22739) FLYING PILOT (POSTHUMOUS)
19. FLT LT GAURAV CHIBBER (22926) FLYING PILOT (POSTHUMOUS)
20. FLT LT KAMBAMPATTI NACHIKETA (22930) FLYING PILOT
21. FG OFFR RAJPAL SINGH DHALIWAL (23535) FLYING PILOT
22. 668396 WO KRISHNA SINGH DHILLON FLIGHT ENGINEER
23. 695490 SGT PASAD PILLA VANKATA NARAYANA RAVI, FLIGHT GUNNER (POSTHUMOUS)
24. 729917 SGT SAHU RAJ KISHORE, FLIGHT ENGINEER (POSTHUMOUS)

Kargil War memorial at Kargil

APPENDIX – I

INSTRUMENT OF ACCESSION OF JAMMU AND KASHMIR STATE DATED 26 OCTOBER 1947

Legal Document No 113

Whereas the Indian Independence Act, 1947, provides that as from the fifteenth day of August, 1947, there shall be set up an independent Dominion known as INDIA, and that the Government of India Act 1935, shall with such omissions, additions, adaptations, and modifications as the Governor General may by order specify, be applicable to the Dominion of India.

And whereas the Government of India Act, 1935, as so adapted by the Governor General, provides that an Indian State may accede to the Dominion of India by an Instrument of Accession executed by the Ruler thereof.

Now, therefore, I Shriman Inder Mahinder Rajrajeswar Maharajadhiraj Shri Hari Singhji, Jammu & Kashmir Naresh Tatha Tibbet adi Deshadhipati, Ruler of Jammu & Kashmir State, in the exercise of my Sovereignty in and over my said State do hereby execute this my Instrument of Accession and

1. I hereby declare that I accede to the Dominion of India with the intent that the Governor General of India, the Dominion Legislature, the Federal Court and any other Dominion authority established for the

purposes of the Dominion shall by virtue of this my Instrument of Accession but subject always to the terms thereof, and for the purposes only of the Dominion, exercise in relation to the State of Jammu & Kashmir (hereinafter referred to as "this State") such functions as may be vested in them by or under the Government of India Act, 1935, as in force in the Dominion of India, on the 15th day of August 1947, (which Act as so in force is hereafter referred to as "the Act").

2. I hereby assume the obligation of ensuring that due effect is given to provisions of the Act within this State so far as they are applicable therein by virtue of this my Instrument of Accession.

3. I accept the matters specified in the schedule hereto as the matters with respect to which the Dominion Legislature may make law for this State.

4. I hereby declare that I accede to the Dominion of India on the assurance that if an agreement is made between the Governor General and the Ruler of this State whereby any functions in relation to the administration in this State of any law of the Dominion Legislature shall be exercised by the Ruler of the State, then any such agreement shall be construed and have effect accordingly.

5. The terms of this my Instrument of Accession shall not be varied by any amendment of the Act or the Indian Independence Act, 1947, unless such amendment is accepted by me by Instrument supplementary to this Instrument.

6. Nothing in this Instrument shall empower the Dominion Legislature to make any law for this State authorizing the compulsory acquisition of land for any purpose, but I hereby undertake that should the Dominion for the purpose of a Dominion law which applies in this State deem it necessary to acquire any land, I will at their request acquire the land at their expense, or, if the land belongs to me transfer it to them on such terms as may be agreed or, in default of agreement, determined by an arbitrator to be appointed by the Chief Justice of India.

7. Nothing in this Instrument shall be deemed to commit in any way to acceptance of any future constitution of India or to fetter my discretion to enter into agreement with the Government of India under any such future constitution.

8. Nothing in this Instrument affects the continuance of my Sovereignty in and over this State, or, save as provided by or under this Instrument, the exercise of any powers, authority and rights now enjoyed by me as Ruler of this State or the validity of any law at present in force in this State.

9. I hereby declare that I execute this Instrument on behalf of this State and that any reference in this Instrument to me or to the Ruler of the State is to be construed as including a reference to my heirs and successors. Given under my hand this 26ᵗʰ day of October, nineteen hundred and forty seven.

Hari Singh
Maharajadhiraj of Jammu and Kashmir State.

Acceptance of Instrument of Accession of Jammu and Kashmir State

Legal Document No 114

I do hereby accept this Instrument of Accession. Dated this twenty-seventh day of October, nineteen hundred and forty seven.

Mountbatten of Burm

Governor General of India

Appendix-II

Resolution 47 (1948)

On the India-Pakistan question submitted jointly by the Representatives for Belgium, Canada, China, Colombia, the United Kingdom, and United States of America and adopted by the Security Council at its 286th meeting held on 21 April 1948.

(Document No. 5/726, dated the 21st April 1948)

THE SECURITY COUNCIL

Having considered the complaint of the Government of India concerning the dispute over the State of Jammu and Kashmir, having heard the representative of India in support of that complaint and the reply and counter complaints of the representative of Pakistan. Being strongly of opinion that the early restoration of peace and order in Jammu and Kashmir is essential and that India and Pakistan should do their utmost to bring about cessation of all fighting. Noting with satisfaction that both India and Pakistan desire that the question of the accession of Jammu and Kashmir to India or Pakistan should be decided through the democratic method of a free and impartial plebiscite, Considering that the continuation of the dispute is likely to endanger international peace and security, Reaffirms its resolution 38 (1948) of 17 January 1948;

Resolves that the membership of the Commission established by its resolution 39 (1948) of 20 January 1948, shall be increased to five and shall include, in addition to the membership mentioned in that Resolution, representatives of... and..., and that if the membership of the Commission has not been completed within ten days from the date the adoption of this resolution the President of the Council may designate such other Member or Members of the United Nations as are required to complete the membership of five; Instructs the Commission to proceed at once to the Indian subcontinent and there place its good offices and mediation at the disposal of the Governments of India and Pakistan with a view to facilitating the taking of the necessary measures, both with respect to the restoration of peace and order and to the holding of a plebiscite by the two (Governments, acting in co-operation with one another and with the Commission, and further instructs the Commission to keep the Council informed of the action taken under the resolution; and, to this end.

Recommends to the Governments of India and Pakistan the following measures as those which in the opinion of the Council and appropriate to bring about a cessation of the lighting and to create proper conditions for a free and impartial plebiscite to decide whether the State of Jammu and Kashmir is to accede to India or Pakistan.

A - RESTORATION OF PEACE AND ORDER

1. The Government of Pakistan should undertake to use its best endeavours:

   (a) To secure the withdrawal from the State of Jammu and Kashmir of tribesmen and Pakistani nationals not normally resident therein who have entered the State for the purposes of fighting, and to prevent any intrusion into the State of such elements and any furnishing of material aid to those fighting in the State;

   (b) To make known to all concerned that the measures indicated in this and the following paragraphs provide full freedom to all subjects of the State, regardless of creed, caste, or party, to express their views and to vote on the question of the accession of the State, and that therefore they should co-operate in the maintenance of peace and order.

2. The Government of India should:

   (a) When it is established to the satisfaction of the Commission set up in accordance with the Council's Resolution 39 (1948) that the tribesmen are withdrawing and that arrangements for the cessation of the fighting have become effective, put into operation in consultation with the Commission a plan for withdrawing their own forces from Jammu and Kashmir and reducing them progressively to the minimum strength required for the support of the civil power in the maintenance of law and order;

(b) Make known that the withdrawal is taking place in stages and announce the completion of each stage; When the Indian forces shall have been reduced to the minimum strength mentioned in (a) above, arrange in consultation with the Commission for the stationing of the remaining forces to be carried out in accordance with the following principles:

(i) That the presence of troops should not afford any intimidation or appearance of intimidation to the inhabitants of the State;

(ii) That as small a number as possible should be retained in forward areas;

(iii) That any reserve of troops which may be included in the total strength should be located within their present base area.

3. The Government of India should agree that until such time as the plebiscite administration referred to below finds it necessary to exercise the powers of direction and supervision over the State forces and policy provided for in paragraph 8, they will be held in areas to be agreed upon with the Plebiscite Administrator.

4. After the plan referred to in paragraph 2 (a) above has been put into operation, personnel recruited locally in each district should so far as possible be utilised for the re-establishment and maintenance of law and order with due regard to protection)t minorities, subject to such additional requirements as may be specified by the Plebiscite Administration referred to in paragraph 7.

5. If these local forces should be found to be inadequate, the Commission, subject to the agreement of both the Government of India and the Government

of Pakistan, should arrange for the use of such forces of either Dominion as it deems t(effective for the purpose of pacification.

B - PLEBISCITE

6. The Government of India should undertake to ensure that the Government of the State invite the major political groups to designate responsible representatives to share equitably and fully in the conduct of the administration at the ministerial level, while the plebiscite is being prepared and carried out.

7. The Government of India should undertake that there will be established in Jammu and Kashmir a Plebiscite Administration to hold a Plebiscite as soon as possible ()n the question of the accession of the State to India or Pakistan.

8. The Government of India should undertake that there will be delegated by the State to the Plebiscite Administration such powers as the latter considers necessary for holding a fair and impartial plebiscite including, for that purpose only, the direction and supervision of the State forces and police.

9. The Government of India should at the request of the Plebiscite Administration, make available from the Indian forces such assistance as the Plebiscite Administration may require for the performance of its functions.

10. (a) The Government of India should agree that a nominee of the Secretary-General of the United Nations will be appointed to be the Plebiscite Administrator. The Plebiscite Administrator, acting as an officer of the State of Jammu and Kashmir, should have authority to nominate the assistants and other subordinates and to draft regulations governing the Plebiscite. Such nominees should be formally appointed and such draft regulations should be formally promulgated by the State of Jammu and Kashmir.

The Government of India should undertake that the Government of Jammu and Kashmir will appoint fully qualified persons nominated by the Plebiscite Administrator to act as special magistrates within the State judicial system to hear cases which in the opinion of the Plebiscite Administrator have a serious bearing on the preparation and the conduct of a free and impartial plebiscite. The terms of service of the Administrator should form the subject of a separate negotiation between the Secretary-General of the United Nations and the Government of India. The Administrator should fix the terms of service for his assistants and subordinates.

The Administrator should have the right to communicate directly, with the Government of the State and with the Commission of the Security Council and, through the Commission, with the Security Council, with the Governments of India and Pakistan and with their representatives with the Commission. It would be his duty to bring to the notice of any or all of the foregoing (as he in his discretion may decide) any circumstances arising which may tend, in his opinion, to interfere with the freedom of the Plebiscite.

11. The Government of India should undertake to prevent to give full support to the Administrator and his staff in preventing any threat, coercion or intimidation, bribery or other undue influence on the voters in the plebiscite, and the Government of India should publicly announce and should cause the Government of the State to announce this undertaking as an international obligation binding on all public authorities and officials in Jammu and Kashmir.

12. The Government of India should themselves and through the Government of the State declare and make known that all subjects of the State of Jammu and Kashmir, regardless of creed, caste or party, will be safe and free in expressing their views and in voting on the question of the accession of the State and that there will be freedom of the Press, speech and assembly and freedom of travel in the State, including freedom of lawful entry and exit.

13. The Government of India should use and should ensure that the Government of the State also use their best endeavour to effect the withdrawal from the State of all Indian nationals other than those who are normally resident therein or who on or since 15ᵗʰ August 1947 have entered it for a lawful purpose.

14. The Government of India should ensure that the Government of the State releases all political prisoners and take all possible steps so that:

(a) all citizens of the State who have left it on account of disturbances are invited and are free to return to their homes and to exercise their rights as such citizens;

(b) there is no victimisation; minorities in all parts of the State are accorded adequate protection.

15. The Commission of the Security Council should at the end of the plebiscite certify to the Council whether the plebiscite has or has not been really free and impartial.

C. GENERAL PROVISIONS

16. The Governments of India and Pakistan should each be invited to nominate a representative to be attached to the Commission for such assistance as it may require in the performance of its task.

17. The Commission should establish in Jammu and Kashmir such observers as it may require of any of the proceedings in pursuance of the measures indicated in the foregoing paragraphs.

18. The Security Council Commission should carry out the tasks assigned to it herein. The Security Council voted on this Resolution on 21-41948 with the following result:

In favour: Argentina, Belgium, Canada, China, France, Syria, U.K. and U.S.A.
Against: None
Abstaining: Belgium, Colombia, Ukrainian S.S.R. and U.S.S.R.

APPENDIX-III

SIMLA AGREEMENT

Agreement on Bilateral Relations between the Government of India and the Government of Pakistan

- The Government of India and the Government of Pakistan are resolved that the two countries put an end to the conflict and confrontation that have hitherto marred their relations and work for the promotion of a friendly and harmonious relationship and the establishment of durable peace in the sub-continent, so that both countries may henceforth devote their resources and energies to the pressing talk of advancing the welfare of their peoples.

- In order to achieve this objective, the Government of India and the Government of Pakistan have agreed as follows:-

  That the principles and purposes of the Charter of the United Nations shall govern the relations between the two countries;

    That the two countries are resolved to settle their differences by peaceful means through bilateral negotiations or by any other peaceful means mutually agreed upon between them. Pending the final settlement of any of the problems between the two countries, neither side shall unilaterally alter the situation and both shall prevent the organization, assistance or encouragement of any acts detrimental to the maintenance of peaceful and harmonious relations;

That the pre-requisite for reconciliation, good neighbor lines and durable peace between them is a commitment by both the countries to peaceful co-existence, respect for each other's territorial integrity and sovereignty and non-interference in each other's internal affairs, on the basis of equality and mutual benefit;

That the basic issues and causes of conflict which have be devilled the relations between the two countries for the last 25 years shall be resolved by peaceful means;

That they shall always respect each other's national unity, territorial integrity, political independence and sovereign equality;

That in accordance with the Charter of the United Nations they will refrain from the threat or use of force against the territorial integrity or political independence of each other.

- Both Governments will take all steps within their power to prevent hostile propaganda directed against each other. Both countries will encourage the dissemination of such information as would promote the development of friendly relations between them.

- In order progressively to restore and normalize relations between the two countries step by step, it was agreed that;

Steps shall be taken to resume communications, postal, telegraphic, sea, land including border posts, and air links including over flights.

Appropriate steps shall be taken to promote travel facilities for the nationals of the other country.

Trade and co-operation in economic and other agreed fields will be resumed as far as possible.

Exchange in the fields of science and culture will be promoted.

- In this connection delegations from the two countries will meet from time to time to work out the necessary details.

- In order to initiate the process of the establishment of durable peace, both the Governments agree that:

Indian and Pakistani forces shall be withdrawn to their side of the international border.

In Jammu and Kashmir, the line of control resulting from the cease-fire of December 17, 1971 shall be respected by both sides without prejudice to the recognized position of either side. Neither side shall seek to alter it unilaterally, irrespective of mutual differences and legal interpretations. Both sides further undertake to refrain from the threat or the use of force in violation of this Line.

The withdrawals shall commence upon entry into force of this Agreement and shall be completed within a period of 30 days thereof.

- This Agreement will be subject to ratification by both countries in accordance with their respective constitutional procedures, and will come into force with effect from the date on which the Instruments of Ratification are exchanged.

- Both Governments agree that their respective Heads will meet again at a mutually convenient time in the future and that, in the meanwhile, the representatives of the two sides will meet to discuss further the modalities and arrangements for the establishment of durable peace and normalization of relations, including the questions of repatriation of prisoners of war and civilian internees, a final settlement of Jammu and Kashmir and the resumption of diplomatic relations.

Sd/-
(Indira Gandhi)
Prime Minister
Republic of India
Sd/-

(Zulfikar Ali Bhutto)
President
Islamic Republic of Pakistan
Simla, the 2ⁿᵈ July, 1972

Appendix-IV

The Lahore Declaration

The following is the text of the Lahore Declaration signed by the Prime Minister, Mr A. B. Vajpayee, and the Pakistan Prime Minister, Mr Nawaz Sharif, in Lahore on Sunday:

The Prime Ministers of the Republic of India and the Islamic Republic of Pakistan:

Sharing a vision of peace and stability between their countries, and of progress and prosperity for their peoples;

Convinced that durable peace and development of harmonious relations and friendly cooperation will serve the vital interests of the peoples of the two countries, enabling them to devote their energies for a better future;

Recognising that the nuclear dimension of the security environment of the two countries adds to their responsibility for avoidance of conflict between the two countries;

Committed to the principles and purposes of the Charter of the United Nations, and the universally accepted principles of peaceful coexistence;

Reiterating the determination of both countries to implementing the Simla Agreement in letter and spirit;

Committed to the objective of universal nuclear disarmament and nonproliferartion;

Convinced of the importance of mutually agreed confidence building measures for improving the security environment;

Recalling their agreement of 23rd September, 1998, that an environment of peace and security is in the supreme national interest of both sides and that the resolution of all outstanding issues, including Jammu and Kashmir, is essential for this purpose;

Have agreed that their respective Governments:

- shall intensify their efforts to resolve all issues, including the issue of Jammu and Kashmir.
- shall refrain from intervention and interference in each other's internal affairs.
- shall intensify their composite and integrated dialogue process for an early and positive outcome of the agreed bilateral agenda.
- shall take immediate steps for reducing the risk of accidental or unauthorised use of nuclear weapons and discuss concepts and doctrines with a view to elaborating measures for confidence building in the nuclear and conventional fields, aimed at prevention of conflict.
- reaffirm their commitment to the goals and objectives of SAARC and to concert their efforts towards the realisation of the SAARC vision for the year 2000 and beyond with a view to promoting the welfare of the peoples of South Asia and to improve their quality of life through accelerated economic growth, social progress and cultural development.
- reaffirm their condemnation of terrorism in all its forms and manifestations and their determination to combat this menace.
- shall promote and protect all human rights and fundamental freedoms.

Signed at Lahore on the 21st day of February 1999.

Atal Behari Vajpayee - Prime Minister of the Republic of India

Muhammad Nawaz Sharif - Prime Minister of the Islamic Republic of Pakistan

APPENDIX-V

JOINT STATEMENT BY PM OF INDIA AND PAKISTAN

The following is the text of the Joint Statement issued at the end of the Prime Minister, Mr. A. B. Vajpayee's visit to Lahore:

In response to an invitation by the Prime Minister of Pakistan, Mr. Muhammad Nawaz Sharif, the Prime Minister of India, Shri Atal Behari Vajpayee, visited Pakistan from 20-21 February, 1999, on the inaugural run of the Delhi-Lahore bus service.

2. The Prime Minister of Pakistan received the Indian Prime Minister at the Wagah border on 20th February 1999. A banquet in honour of the Indian Prime Minister and his delegation was hosted by the Prime Minister of Pakistan at Lahore Fort, on the same evening. Prime Minister, Atal Behari Vajpayee, visited Minar-e- Pakistan, Mausoleum of Allama Iqabal, Gurudawara Dera Sahib and Samadhi of Maharaja Ranjeet Singh. On 21st February, a civic reception was held in honour of the visiting Prime Minister at the Governor's House.

3. The two leaders held discussions on the entire range of bilateral relations, regional cooperation within SAARC, and issues of international concern. They decided that:

(a) The two Foreign Ministers will meet periodically to discuss all issues of mutual concern, including nuclear related issues.

(b) The two sides shall undertake consultations on WTO related issues with a view to coordinating their respective positions.

(c) The two sides shall determine areas of cooperation in Information Technology, in particular for tackling the problems of Y2K.

(d) The two sides will hold consultations with a view to further liberalising the visa and travel regime.

(e) The two sides shall appoint a two member committee at ministerial level to examine humanitarian issues relating to Civilian detainees and missing POWs.

4. They expressed satisfaction on the commencement of a Bus Service between Lahore and New Delhi, the release of fishermen and civilian detainees and the renewal of contacts in the field of sports.

5. Pursuant to the directive given by the two Prime Ministers, the Foreign Secretaries of Pakistan and India signed a Memorandum of Understanding on 21st February 1999, identifying measures aimed at promoting an environment of peace and security between the two countries.

6. The two Prime Ministers signed the Lahore Declaration embodying their shared vision of peace and stability between their countries and of progress and prosperity for their peoples.

7. Prime Minister, Atal Behari Vajpayee extended an invitation to Prime Minister, Muhammad Nawaz Sharif, to visit India on mutually convenient dates.

8. Prime Minister, Atal Behari Vajpayee, thanked Prime Minister, Muhammad Nawaz Sharif, for the warm welcome and gracious hospitality extended to him and members of his delegation and for the excellent arrangements made for his visit.

Lahore,
February 21, 1999

APPENDIX VI

FEBRUARY 21, 1999
MEMORANDUM OF UNDERSTANDING

The following is the text of the Memorandum of Understanding signed by the Foreign Secretary, Mr K. Raghcunath, and the Pakistan Foreign Secretary, Mr Shamshad Ahmad, in Lahore on Sunday:

The Foreign Secretaries of India and Pakistan:

Reaffirming the continued commitment of their respective governments to the principles and purposes of the U.N. Charter;

Reiterating the determination of both countries to implementing the Shimla Agreement in letter and spirit;

Guided by the agreement between their Prime Ministers of 23rd September 1998 that an environment of peace and security is in the supreme national interest of both sides and that resolution of all outstanding issues, including Jammu and Kashmir, is essential for this purpose;

Pursuant to the directive given by their respective Prime Ministers in Lahore, to adopt measures for promoting a stable environment of peace, and security between the two countries;

Have on this day, agreed to the following:-

- The two sides shall engage in bilateral consultations on security concepts, and nuclear doctrines, with a view to developing measures for confidence building in the nuclear and coventional fields, aimed at avoidance of conflict.

- The two sides undertake to provide each other with advance notification in respect of ballistic missile flight tests, and shall conclude a bilateral agreement in this regard.
- The two sides are fully committed to undertaking national measures to reducing the risks of accidental or unauthorised use of nuclear weapons under their respective control. The two sides further undertake to notify each, other immediately in the event of any accidental, unauthorised or unexplained incident that could create the risk of a fallout with adverse consequences for both sides, or an outbreak of a nuclear war between the two countries, as well as to adopt measures aimed at diminishing the possibility of such actions, or such incidents being misinterpreted by the other. The two side shall identify/establish the appropriate communication mechanism for this purpose.
- The two sides shall continue to abide by their respective unilateral moratorium on conducting further nuclear test explosions unless either side, in exercise of its national sovereignty decides that extraordinary events have jeopardised its supreme interests.
- The two sides shall conclude an agreement on prevention of incidents at sea in order to ensure safety of navigation by naval vessels, and aircraft belonging to the two sides.
- The two sides shall periodically review the implementation of existing Confidence Building Measures (CBMs) and where necessary, set up appropriate consultative mechanisms to monitor and ensure effective implementation of these CBMs.
- The two sides shall undertake a review of the existing communication links (e.g. between the respective Directors- General, Military Operations) with a view to upgrading and improving these links, and to provide for fail-safe and secure communications.
- The two sides shall engage in bilateral consultations on security, disarmament and non-proliferation issues within the context of negotiations on these issues in multilateral fora.

Where required, the technical details of the above measures will be worked out by experts of the two sides in meetings to be held on mutually agreed dates, before mid 1999, with a view to reaching bilateral agreements.

Done at Lahore on 21ˢᵗ February 1999 in the presence of Prime Minister of India, Mr. Atal Behari Vajpayee, and Prime Minister of Pakistan, Mr. Muhammad Nawaz Sharif.

(K. Raghunath)
Foreign Secretary of the Republic of India

(Shamshad Ahmad)
Foreign Secretary of the Islamic Republic of Pakistan

APPENDIX-VII

JOINT STATEMENT OF NAWAZ SHARIF AND US PRESIDENT CLINTON AT BLAIR HOUSE ON WITHDRAWAL OF PAKISTAN ARMY (JULY 4, 1999)

President Clinton and Prime Minister Sharif share the view that the current fighting in the Kargil region of Kashmir is dangerous and contains the seeds of a wider conflict. They also agreed that it was vital for the peace of south Asia that the Line of Control in Kashmir be respected by both parties, in accordance with their 1972 Simla Accord. It was agreed between the President and the Prime Minister that concrete steps will be taken for the restoration of the line of control in accordance with the Simla Agreement. The President urged an immediate cessation of the hostilities once these steps are taken. The Prime Minister and president agreed that the bilateral dialogue begun in Lahore in February provides the best forum for resolving all issues dividing India and Pakistan, including Kashmir. The President said he would take a personal interest in encouraging an expeditious resumption and intensification of those bilateral efforts, once the sanctity of the Line of Control has been fully restored. The President reaffirmed his intent to pay an early visit to South Asia.

NOTE: An original was not available for verification of the content of this joint statement.

ABBREVIATIONS

1	33 FF	33 Frontier Force
2	Adm	Administration
3	AGPL	Actual Ground Position Line
4	AK-47	Automatic Kalashnikov
5	Art.	Artillery
6	ASST LDR	Assistant Leader
7	AVM	Ati Vishisht Seva Medal
8	BBC	British Broadcasting Corporation
9	Bde	Brigadier
10	BJP	Bharatiya Janata Party
11	Bn	Battalion
12	Bns	Battalions
13	CFL	Cease Fire Line
14	CO	Commanding Officer
15	Capt	Captain
16	CAS	Chief of the Air Staff
17	CBM	Confidence Building Measure
18	CCS	Cabinet Committee on Security
19	CDOS	Commandos
20	CDR	Commander
21	CHM	Company Havildar Major
22	CI	Counter-Insurgency
23	CIA	Central Intelligence Agency

24	COAS	Chief of Army Staff
25	COSC	Chief of Staff Committee
26	COY	Company
27	CPASS	Centre for Peace A Security Studies
28	Det	Detachment
29	DG	Director General
30	DGMO	Director General of Military Operations
31	DIST.	District
32	DVSN	Division
33	F O O	Forward Observation Officer
34	FCNA	Force Commander Northern Area
35	Fd Regt	Field Regiment
36	FG-OFFR	Flying Officer
37	FLT LT	Flight Lieutenant
38	GARH	Garhwal Rifles
39	Gen	General
40	GHQ	General Health Questionnaire
41	GNR	Gunner
42	GOC	General Officer Commanding
43	GOC	General Officer Commanding
44	Govt.	Government
45	GP CAPT	Group Captain
46	GR	Gorkha Rifles
47	GREN	Grenadier
48	Grp	Group
49	H A P O	High Altitude Pulmonary Oedema
50	H Q	Headquarters
51	HAV	Havildar
52	HU	Helicopter Unit
53	Hvy Mor Regt	Heavy Mortar Regiment
54	IAF	Indian Air Force
55	IB	Intelligence Bureau
56	INS	Indian Naval Ship

57	ISI	Inter Services Intelligence
58	J&K	Jammu and Kashmir
59	JAK RIF	Jammu and Kashmir Rifles
60	JAKLI	Jammu and Kashmir Light Infantry
61	JCO	Junior Commanding Officer
62	JD(H)	Joint Director (Helicopter)
63	KM	Kilometre
64	KPVT	Krupnokaliberniy Pulemyot Vladimirova Tank
65	KRC	Kargil Review Committee
66	L/NK	Lance Naik
67	LMG	Light Machine Gun
68	LOC	Line Of Control
69	LRP	Long Range Patrols
70	Lt	Lieutenant
71	Lt Col	Multi Barrel Rocket Launcher
72	Lt Gen	Lieutenant General
73	Lt Regt	Light Regiment
74	Maj	Major
75	MBRL	Multi Barrel Rocket Launcher
76	MEA	Ministry of External Affairs
77	Med Regt	Medium Regiment
78	MMG	Medium Machine Gun
79	Mnt	Mountain
80	Mnt Art Brgd	Mountain Artillery Brigade
81	MOD	Ministry of Defence
82	MOU	Memorandum of Understanding
83	N L T	Northern Light Infantry
84	NB	Naib
85	NDA	National Democratic Alliance
86	NH	National Highway
87	NK	Naik
88	NSC	National Security Council

89	NSG	National Security Guard
90	OP	Observation Post
91	OP	Operation
92	ORBAT	Order of Battle
93	P M	Prime Minister
94	PAF	Pakistani Air Force
95	Para	Parachute
96	Pep	Junior Commanding Officer
97	PNVD	Passive Night Vision Device
98	POK	Pak Occupied Kashmir
99	POW	Prisoner of War
100	PVC	Param Vir Chakra
101	PVSM	Param Vishisht Seva Medal
102	R R	Rashtriya Rifles
103	RAJ RIF	Rajputana Rifles
104	RAW	Research and Analysis Wing
105	Rckt Regt	Rocket Regiment
106	Recon & Obs Sqdr	Reconnaissance and Observation Squadron
107	RFN	Rifleman
108	RIF	Rifles
109	RPG	Rocket Propelled Grenade
110	RPG	Rocket Propelled Grenade
111	S S B	Service Selection Board
112	S S G	Special Services Group
113	S S H	Subsector Haneef
114	SAARC	South Asian Association for Regional Cooperation
115	SEP	Sepoy
116	SIGMN	Signal Man
117	SIND	Sindh
118	SPG	Special Protection Group
119	SPR	Sapper

120	Sq. Km.	Square Kilometre
121	Sqdrn	Squadron
122	Sqn LDR	Squadron Leader
123	SUB	Subedar
124	TNT	Trinitrotoluene
125	UMG	U B E R Machine gun
126	UN	United Nations
127	UNCIP	United Nations Commission for Indian & Pakistan
128	UNMOGIP	United Nations Military Observer Group in India and Pakistan
129	UNMOGIP	United Nations Military Observer Group in India & Pakistan
130	UNO	United Nations Organisation
131	USA	United States of America
132	VCOAS	Vice Chief of Army Staff
133	VSM	Vishisht Seva Medal
134	WASO	Winter Air Surveillance Operations
135	WG	Wing Commander
136	WTO	World Trade Organisation
137	Y2K	Year 2000

BIBLIOGRAPHY

1. Kargil From Surprise to Victory, General V. P. Malik, HarperCollins Publishers India
2. Dateline Kargil, Gaurav C Sawant, Macmillan
3. Asymmetric Warfare in South Asia, Peter R. Lavoy, Cambridge University Press
4. Beyond NJ 9842 The Siachen Saga, Nitin A. Gokhale, Bloomsbury India
5. Limited Conflict Under the Nuclear Umbrella: Indian and Pakistani Lessons–From the Kargil Crisis, Ashley J. Tellis; Christine Fair; Jamison Jo Medby, RAND; NSRD
6. Weapons of Peace: The Secret Story of India's Quest to be a Nuclear Power, Raj Chengappa
7. In Service of Emergent India A Call To Honor, Jaswant Singh, Indiana University Press
8. The Kargil War, Praveen Swami, Left Word
9. This Unquiet Land Stories From India's Fault Lines, Barkha Dutt, Aleph
10. Kargil: Blood on the Snow Tactical Victory Strategic Failure, Maj Gen Ashok Kalyan Verma AVSM, Manohar
11. From Surprise to Reckoning, The Kargil Review Committee Report, Sage Publications
12. Indian Army Order of Battle, Richard A. Rinaldi and Ravi Rikhye, Tiger Lily Books

13. Artillery: The Battle-Winning Arm, Major General Jagjit Singh (Retd.), Lancer Publishers & Distributors

14. Despatches From Kargil, Srinjoy Chowdhury, Penguin Books

15. The Brave, Rachna Bisht Rawat, Penguin Books

16. Systematic Geography of Jammu and Kashmir, Majid Husain, Rawat Publications

17. Kagil Turning the Tide, Lt Gen Mohinder Puri; PVSM; UYSM, Lancer

18. Kargil Revisited Images And Perceptions Of The Kargil War After Ten Years, M. Neelamalar, Shubhi Publications

19. War Ethics And The Kargil Crisis, Sita Ram Sharma, Book Enclave

20. Hero of Batalik Param Veer Chakra: Capt Manoj Kr. Pandey, Pawan Kumar Mishra, VL Media Solutions

21. Engaging India: Diplomacy, Democracy and the Bomb by Strobe Talbott

22. Guns and Yellow Roses: Eassays on the Kargil War, Sankarshan Thakur, Harpercollins India

23. India at Risk, Jashwant Singh, Rainlight- Rupa.

24. India's Military Conflicts and Diplomac, Gen V. P. Malik, Harper

25. The Kargil war 1999, Brig (Prof) B. S. Joshi, Surendra Publication

26. From Hydaspes to Kargil, A history of Warfare in India, Kaushik Roy, Manohar

27. India's Military Conflicts and Diplomacy, Gen V.P. Malik, Harper Collins

Printed in the United States
By Bookmasters